The Assertive Practitioner

How a staff team works together and how effective and cohesive they are impacts significantly on the children that they care for as well as having implications for the general early years practice and the success of the business of the setting. Drawing together theory and practice, this book provides comprehensive guidance on assertive communication and offers a range of clear, practical strategies that are easy to implement in the early years setting.

The Assertive Practitioner aims to distinguish between assertive, passive, aggressive and passive aggressive communication so that early years practitioners can gain confidence, become more self-aware, reflect on their own practice and develop their effective communication skills. Divided into three parts, 'what is assertiveness?', 'using it' and 'developing it', the authors consider the skills of good communication and assertiveness in the early years setting, offering practical guidance on:

- recruitment, induction, ongoing staff training and supervision;
- disciplinary processes including handling difficult conversations and refocusing a team after a critical incident;
- staff relationships with parents and other professionals;
- involving the team in problem solving and implementing change;
- engaging with the community;
- how to get support for yourself as a manager.

Packed full of practical strategies and case studies, this timely new book will be invaluable support for all those wanting to enhance and improve professional practice and relationships in the early years setting.

Deborah Price is Senior Lecturer at the University of Brighton and an Associate Lecturer at The Open University, UK. She has worked in early and primary years as a teacher, trainer, inspector and lecturer.

Cathy Ota works across the UK and internationally as an Independent Education Consultant and Team Dynamics Specialist. She is Co-founder and Director of Working With Others, a training programme for building relational intelligence for staff teams and children in schools and early years settings.

The Assertive Practitioner

How to improve early years practice through effective communication

Deborah Price and
Cathy Ota

Routledge
Taylor & Francis Group

LONDON AND NEW YORK

British Library Cataloguing in Publication Data
A catalogue record for this book is available from the British Library

Library of Congress Cataloging in Publication Data
Names: Ota, Cathy, author. | Price, Deborah, author.
Title: The assertive practitioner : how to improve early years practice
    through effective communication / Cathy Ota and Deborah Price.
Description: Abingdon, Oxon ; New York, NY : Routledge, [2016]
Identifiers: LCCN 2015021218| ISBN 9781138832312 (hbk) |
    ISBN 9781138832329 (pbk) | ISBN 9781315665337 (ebk)
Subjects: LCSH: Communication in education. | Teaching—Practice. |
    Effective teaching. | Assertiveness (Psychology)
Classification: LCC LB1033.5 .O83 2016 | DDC 371.102/2—dc23
LC record available at http://lccn.loc.gov/2015021218

ISBN: 978-1-138-83231-2 (hbk)
ISBN: 978-1-138-83232-9 (pbk)
ISBN: 978-1-315-66533-7 (ebk)

Typeset in Sabon
by Swales & Willis Ltd, Exeter, Devon, UK
Printed by Ashford Colour Press Ltd.

Dedication

Deborah: For my dear friend Sheena Rogers

Cathy: For my brothers and sisters, Tony, Tammy, Jim,
Colette, Frances and Bernadette

Contents

Acknowledgements

Central to this book, particularly the case studies, are all the children, families, practitioners and students we have worked with over many years. We are enormously grateful to them for sharing their stories. Deborah would like to especially thank Maria Jastrzebska for her help with assertion techniques, Allie Rogers for case study inspiration and colleagues in the School of Education at the University of Brighton. Cathy would like to especially thank Mary Pat Vollick, Alison Dearden and James Lemon for their help with understanding and exploring assertiveness, constructive conflict and difficult conversations.

Introduction

Being assertive is about communicating clearly and cleanly. Being assertive is not about being selfish or aggressive. It is not about getting one's own way all the time or always being able to 'win' in an argument or confrontation. It is also not about learning a package of skills or tactics that will enable one to manipulate or control the people encountered in the workplace.

In exploring the key elements of assertive communication and offering a range of clear, easy to use, practical strategies, this book will highlight how assertiveness is a key component in enhancing and improving professional practice and relationships in early years.

This book aims to distinguish between assertive, passive, aggressive and passive aggressive communication. In this way through a greater awareness and understanding of what each style looks like and how to combat it, early years practitioners at all levels can gain confidence by becoming more self-aware, reflect on their own communication styles and develop their skills in effective professional communication.

We start by examining why assertiveness is especially useful in an early years setting. We look at how assertive behavior can be misinterpreted and feared in an early years ethos. We work through the theory and practice of assertiveness and detail a simple three-point plan for practitioners to try in the workplace. We then move through the roles that practitioners have in an early years setting and describe, through the use of case studies, how assertive behaviour can work effectively as contrasted with aggressive or passive reactions to difficult situations.

We also look at the benefits of conflict. Practitioners can adopt passive or passive aggressive strategies in the mistaken belief that conflict should be avoided in an early years setting at all costs. That it is somehow an anathema to the ethos of working in a caring nurturing way with children. In fact we intend to show that healthy conflict and resolution of difficulties is the opposite of this. Dealt with in a congruent and positive way the management of conflict and difficult conversations can provide a healthy role model to children. It can also energise and focus a team to be accountable to each other and challenge poor practice in a way that is supportive and works towards the setting's vision statement.

Two important points that we need to make and that have to be seen in the context of this book.

Firstly, that underpinning all of this assertive practice is a desire to improve the welfare and experiences of children. Modelling healthy relationships between adults is one of the responsibilities that practitioners have. One of the ways that children learn how to be adults is by observing the people around them. It seems obvious to note that if they see adults behaving in an aggressive way – shouting, having rows, storming out of rooms – then they will internalise that this is acceptable behaviour and that aggressive strategies are approved of.

What seems less obvious is that more passive behaviour is also noticed by children. This can include: gossiping about someone then falling silent when they come into a room, feeling very angry towards someone but not saying anything, letting body language express the emotion by moving resources around angrily, behaving with the children in a curt way or trying to compensate by being overly bright. All these actions that practitioners believe are part of 'not saying anything' or 'not letting it affect my work'. All of these passive aggressive behaviours will be noted by children.

Not only will it surround them with an air of unease and a feeling that something is wrong, but it will also be noted as an approved way of expressing adult feelings.

The second point we want to make is that all of the ways of dealing with work situations that we discuss in this book can be transferred to practitioners' home life. Assertive techniques are just as effective with partners, friends and family as they are in work situations. Indeed we would suggest that it is inevitable that when practitioners start to modify and change their behaviour at work by exploring the three step plan then that will spill over into their social and family life as they seek to feel congruent.

Summary of chapters

We haven't intended for this book to be read in strict chapter order throughout. We would suggest though, that it is important that the chapters in section one should be read first in order to provide a good grounding and understanding of assertion techniques. Practitioners could then read the chapter that best describes their work situation and role. The final section could be read in any order and out of further interest to think about children and assertive behaviour, developing an assertive team and further work with embedding assertiveness in practice.

PART ONE: WHAT IS ASSERTIVENESS?

Chapter 1: Why assertiveness is important for early years teams

This chapter will establish why assertiveness, as an aspect of effective communication, is a crucial element of good professional practice for early years practitioners and managers. It will explore how assertiveness tools can offer an important and valuable tool for addressing and managing conflict, as well as developing and improving early years settings. It will also explore how the specific culture and ethos of many early years teams and settings can work against encouraging and enabling assertiveness.

It is not that the best teams never have conflict, it is that they are able to deal with it and move on together. Conflict offers the opportunity for constructive debate, it can enable a team to reflect, improve and develop. Conflict is an inevitable part of life, teams and organisations, including early years ones. Why is it, then, that conflict is rarely explicit, acknowledged and often avoided in early years, that is until it escalates and explodes? We believe that fear is at the root of this, as is lack of confidence in the skills or ability to know what to say or do when confronted with the myriad of emotions, behaviours and thoughts that can arise when conflict bubbles to the surface.

Drawing on different examples from other public and private sector organisations, the chapter will demonstrate how this can be especially difficult to confront and contend with in early years teams. One reason for this, we believe, is the general culture and ethos of most early years settings that is infused with nurturing, caring and general niceness. This may also be seen as compounded by a predominantly female workforce where 'niceness' and 'not rocking the boat' is reinforced rather than speaking out and being labeled a 'troublemaker' or 'difficult person'.

This chapter will set out how assertiveness is a practical strategy that can benefit many aspects of early years professional practice and organisations; within staff teams; between managers and their staff; as a role model for children and in communicating with other professionals, outside agencies and parents, carers and families.

Chapter 2: What is assertiveness?

Having located assertiveness as a communication tool within the context of early years, this chapter will identify the elements of assertiveness as part of a repertoire of effective communication skills. Drawing on theoretical underpinnings such as Piaget, Vygotsky, Object Relations Theory, this chapter will compare assertiveness with passive, aggressive and passive aggressive communication styles, including a focus on the aims, personal perceptions and outcomes of each approach. Building on Chapter 1, assertiveness will be discussed within the broader context of conflict as a positive aspect of organisations and teams and disagreeing respectfully and politely.

Chapter 3: The structure of assertiveness communication – how to do it

Having set the context of early years and assertiveness theory, this chapter will present the practicalities of assertive techniques and offer a 'how to' guide based on a simple three-step approach. It will discuss both verbal and nonverbal aspects of assertiveness and make the important distinction between this and passive aggressive behaviour. A case study will be used as an illustration.

PART TWO: USING IT

This section of the book will employ a case study approach to illustrate how assertiveness can be used by a range of early years professionals: the early years manager, room leader and practitioner. With case study examples this section will take each role in turn and consider where and how assertiveness can be used in terms of: specifics for the role; practical tactics to use; what if you don't get what you want; as part of ongoing good practice (rather than reactive crisis management).

Chapter 4: Assertiveness for the early years practitioner

Using the general framework set out in the introduction to Section 2, this chapter will focus on the general early years practitioner. Specifically for this role it will highlight how assertiveness can be used effectively with colleagues, parents and carers, and as a role model for children. It will offer assertiveness as a means of establishing a professional role and identity within a team, working with other colleagues and a manager. It will offer practical ideas for tackling passive and passive aggressive behaviour in others. The case study will especially focus on relationships with parents and the tension between thinking of parents as the purchasers of a service that the setting is selling and professional values and integrity.

Chapter 5: Assertiveness for the early years room leader

Showing how assertive techniques can help, this chapter will acknowledge how early years practitioners in this role generally take on some management responsibility and additionally are required to respond to their manager. They are also more frequently involved with conversations, sometimes sensitive or difficult ones, with parents. The case study will concentrate on the issues that can arise when a colleague is promoted to room leader over another colleague.

Chapter 6: Assertiveness for the early years manager

This chapter will continue to build on the strategies and areas covered in Chapters 4 and 5, this time moving on to consider how assertiveness can support early years managers. The chapter will look at the aspects of managing and leading staff including discipline, hiring, supervision, team meetings and team building, taking change forward, leading with a vision and working with other agencies, Ofsted and multi-agency working. These are all specifically relevant to this role.

PART THREE: DEVELOPING IT

Having set out the key elements of assertiveness and shown how it works for different early years roles and responsibilities, this section will develop and extend the further possibilities that assertiveness offers for improving teams and communication between individuals and settings.

Chapter 7: Equipping children with the skills

Offering a range of practical ideas and activities, this chapter will focus on how assertiveness can be introduced to young children. Establishing this as a valuable aspect of best practice for early years it will argue that assertiveness offers important skills for children as they learn to communicate and interact with their peers and adults around them.

Chapter 8: Developing the broader climate

This chapter will consider how confidence and skills in assertiveness, as well as more effective communication can be achieved in early years teams by addressing and being mindful of the broader climate and environment of the organisation. This chapter will discuss how teams can be empowered and enriched through attention to building trust and respect, sharing a vision and developing joint ownership. Presenting a range of ideas for both the general early years practitioner and leader/manager it will demonstrate how attention to simple strategies such as knowing and using names, eye contact, and basic listening skills can be employed to create a climate where assertiveness can flourish positively and productively.

Chapter 9: Embedding, sustaining and developing assertiveness in your practice and setting

This chapter will address both the role and responsibilities of the general early years practitioner and leader/manager. Building on the foundation and basic assertiveness techniques offered this chapter would present a range of ideas and possibilities for further developing and using these skills in professional practice. It will offer practical activities that can be used with staff teams to introduce and extend assertiveness skills and confidence among a staff team. This moves on from the techniques that are explored in Chapter 6 as these are more about one to one assertion. Here we are looking at cascading assertion tools so that a whole team and be skilled up in techniques. In this way assertion doesn't just rest with individuals but becomes part of the settings' ethos.

CONCLUSION

Here we draw the threads of the book together and think about the ways forward for early years practitioners and teams. We also explore the ways that this assertiveness practice can impact on practitioner's personal and family life and the benefits of this.

List of additional resources

Dickenson, A. and Charlesworth, K. (2002), 'A woman in your own right', London: Quartet.
Gawinski, G. and Graessle, L. (1999), 'Planning together: The art of effective teamwork', London: Bedford Press.

Websites

http://lulastic.co.uk/activism/parenting-for-social-justice-non-violent-communication/

Part 1

What is assertiveness?

Chapter 1

Why assertiveness is important for early years teams

This chapter is about the importance of using assertiveness skills in early years and examines why it is especially important to use these skills in the early years sector.

The main points in this chapter are that

* Women make up the majority of the early years workforce, often in part-time and low-paid positions.
* There are a small amount of men in the workforce.
* Because of the idea that working with children is naturally 'women's work' men in childcare encounter a lot of suspicion and prejudice.
* Because of these reasons assertion skills are important for both women and men in childcare in order to bolster up their self-esteem and manage difficult conversations.

Men in childcare

Before we talk about the importance of using assertion skills in early years we need to state in advance that in this chapter we will mainly be talking about the importance of assertion skills for women in early years. We know that this may seem like an assumption and we also acknowledge the importance of assertion skills for men in childcare. Statistics (from 2012) show that only 2% of the early years' workforce is male. Assertion skills are important for anyone to understand and take into their practice. We do feel that it is especially important for women who work in an area of the workforce that has historically been undervalued and is low paid, often part time work. We also wanted in this section to extend this to include men in childcare, as there are also pressures and expectations of them that mean that challenging attitudes and having difficult conversations using assertion techniques is essential practice.

The Pre-school Learning Alliance carried out a survey in 2011 that showed that, although most parents surveyed said that they were happy for men to care for their children, this number decreased the younger the children were.

> The survey of 1,200 mothers and fathers who use childcare found that almost all (97.9 per cent) parents are happy for men to work with children aged three to five in day nurseries.
>
> However, the percentage of parents fell to 89 per cent when it came to younger children aged from birth to two. Of the remaining 11 per cent, only 3.2 per cent of parents were unhappy for men to work with such young children.
>
> (Baker, 2012)

The survey went onto interview male school leavers and ask them why they weren't considering early years as a career option and the answers ranged from it being 'women's work' to worrying what other people would think of them and lack of career progression.

We think that the small amount of men who do work in early years need and would benefit from assertion skills. They have to take engage with and challenge the attitudes of some of the women that they work with 'why would you want to work with babies?' and also the prejudices and suspicions of some of the parents. One of the men that we have interviewed for our previous book on leadership talked about starting work in an early years setting:

> When I started work there it felt like a bit of a closed shop. For a while I was the only man working there and I was always conscious of the other women judging me and wondering why I was working there. I felt the pressure to be even better than my best and never make a mistake. There was also the attitude of the parents. One mother openly made some comments about paedophiles and I didn't know what to do. I knew that my manager had taken a risk hiring me and had to speak to quite a few parents about my placement in the baby room and I didn't want to add to her stress. Once another man was employed there things got a bit better even though he just works in the after school club. I still resent being the one who is expected to do all of the

odd jobs in the nursery, like moving heavy furniture and changing light bulbs. They seem to look to me to take the initiative in outside play as well. I have heard quite a few staff members refer to us as 'the boys' and I feel uncomfortable with that but don't know what to do'.

(‘Tom’, baby room practitioner)

It can be argued that men have an inbuilt assertion in the workplace that comes from their place in society and the way that they and their work are treated and that there is no need for them to learn additional skills. This can stem from the societal assumption, still prevalent, that men need to work and have a career in order to support their families while for women part time work has to fit in around childcare responsibilities and provide 'pin money' (think about the meaning behind that expression).

In the annual survey of hours and earnings 2013 these assumptions are shown to be a harsh reality and prove that, although women's wages have increased (and it could be noted that this may just be because the minimum wage rate has increased), the gap between men and women's wages is actually getting bigger.

- For men, full-time earnings were £556 per week, up 1.8%, compared with £459 for women, up 2.2%.
- The gender pay gap (i.e. the difference between men's and women's earnings as a percentage of men's earnings) based on median gross hourly earnings (excluding overtime) for full-time employees increased to 10.0% from 9.5% in 2012 (Office for National Statistics, 2013).

Even taking this into account, there are specific reasons why men in early years childcare still need support with assertion skills.

Background to the early years sector

We attempt below to provide a short summary of the most recent – post 1989 – changes to the early years sector and workforce and show this as context for the importance of assertion skills in the current climate and regime. Since the Children Act 1989 and the move towards greater regulation of early years provision there has also been a corresponding shift towards increasing the professional status of early years workers.

Historically, as we have already discussed, the people who work in early years settings have been part time, low-paid workers and stereotypically the work itself has been seen as little more than baby-sitting. Society has seen the raising of children, whether at home or in day care settings, to be 'women's work' and an extension of the naturally caring and nurturing role that women are often expected to fill. The Coalition Governments' publication 'More Great Childcare' 2013 states that:

> Low wages for staff working in the early years limit the scope for further professionalisation, with many staff paid little more than the minimum wage. In 2011, the national minimum wage for those over 21 was £6.08 an hour. Those working below supervisor level in full daycare settings earn on average only slightly more than this, at £6.60 an hour.
>
> (Department for Education, 2013, p. 13)

However, post 1989 early years as a sector has been more regulated, more monitored and there has also been an interest in early years at Government level led by the Sure Start initiative. This interest in early years and the benefit of investing in it formed one of the opening statements of the Tickell review in 2011. This review led to the reformulation of the EYFS in 2014.

> Investment and interventions in the early years are generally more effective in improving outcomes than investments and interventions later in life. The return on public investment in high quality early years education is substantial leading to decreased social problems, reduced inequality and increased productivity and GDP growth.
>
> (Department for Education, 2011, p. 11)

The range of professional qualifications available to practitioners has increased dramatically in recent years. This was matched initially with generous funding from Local Authorities in order to support and enable practitioners to complete higher-level training and foundation degree levels of higher education. This funding has now tailed off with local authority cut backs and also the introduction and availability to part time students of the government student loan scheme. For a few years however, with this funding, there was a really positive influx of women who used the financial support to access the education that they had disengaged with as young people. They were now able to reclaim this education through their part time work with children. The early years sector was their route to academic success and many students went on and achieved full BA honours while working and having their study part funded by local authorities.

Post 1996 with the 'nursery voucher' scheme initiated by the Conservative government and then replaced in 1997 with the incoming Labour Government's nursery education scheme .the number of private day nurseries increased dramatically. Provision was also added to by the expansion of the Sure Start project from areas to deprivation initially to become the UK wide (3631 in 2010) children's centres that offered a universal service based in local authorities.

More recently the new qualification of EYT (early years teacher) has been launched. This follows on from the previous EYP (early years professional). This new EYT has the same requirements as a primary teacher with QTS (qualified teacher status). Holders of EYT, before completing the qualification, are expected to hold a degree and also have achieved a grade C or above (or comparable) in maths, English and science. The Coalition Government foresee early years care and education being led by early years teachers in the future. Their reasoning for this is that with higher qualified staff comes more flexibility and so higher staff:child ratios. We would not agree with this reasoning as our argument is that having staff who are professionally trained does not transfer to the idea that this means that they can manage larger groups of children.

We discuss in Chapter 2 of our earlier book *Leading and Supporting Early Years Teams* how this move towards enhanced professionalism has also bought with it an expectation of higher qualifications within the staff team in settings. It is currently expected that at least half the staff in an early years setting are qualified to level two and above.

The Nutbrown review of children's services that 'More Great Childcare' refers to recommended that: The EYFS requirements should be revised so that, from September 2013, a minimum of 50 per cent of staff in group settings need to possess at least a 'full and relevant' Level 3 to count in the staff:child ratios. Nutbrown also recommends that there should be further revision so that, from September 2015, a minimum of 70 per cent of staff in group settings need to possess at least a 'full and relevant' Level 3 to count in the staff:child ratios. This has not been acted on in the most recent revision of the EYFS (Department of Education, 2013).

What does all this mean?

We feel that there have been great moves forward with the recent interest in early years and renewed understanding of the importance of this work. The practitioners in early years settings are undertaking, what we would argue, is the most important job in society, that of educating and caring for the next generation and enabling parents and carers to work. Underpinning this rise in regulatory standards and the overseeing of quality of provision in early years settings is the idea that children are getting a better experience in settings and a positive start to education, taking the definition of education in a holistic way, as in including social and emotional development. Early years provision in the UK has the double edged aim of providing children with the best possible start in life and also providing safe and affordable care for the workforce in order that parents can work and contribute to the economy. In addition to this the majority of nurseries are privately owned small businesses and are in competition with each other. The two aims do not always agree with each other, as what is affordable is not always good quality.

Providing quality education and care provision cannot be done 'on the cheap'. We believe that the greatest asset that a setting has are its staff team and this is where the money should be channeled. There is a tension in small businesses to attract the 'customer', that is the parent, by providing a quality provision. At present this quality is measured by OFSTED, but also by parents' perceptions of what should be present. Both agencies prefer there to be a low turnover of staff in order to provide continuity to the children and a stable staff team. In order to do this staff need to be encouraged to remain in the setting by offering an attractive wages package. Despite this reasoning high staff turnover is a worrying issue in the early years sector and we think that the wages are still not attractive enough to keep staff in position and encourage them, not only to remain in the workforce, but to seek promotion and higher qualifications.

The situation at present is that the sector is seeing the benefits of increased provision, a structured play based curriculum and the expectation of a qualified and professional workforce led and managed by practitioners who have the knowledge and skills of teachers. There is with that, we feel, an added stress and workload burden on practitioners without the enhancement that status and pay can bring.

> Why should I take all this paperwork home with me to do in my own time? I have staff phoning in sick with stress, parents refusing to pay their bills, OFSTED on my back wanting me to fill in a mountain of forms and the nursery owner going on at me to keep the costs down and stop ordering expensive paper and paints. I could earn about the same answering the phone in my local dentist, and have none of the hassle.
>
> (Nursery manager, interviewed in 2013)

This is where assertion skills are crucial in order to manage this enhanced role effectively and gain maximum job satisfaction. We are not saying that assertion skills will redress the gender pay gap or the low pay in the early years sector. What we will notice though is that people working in childcare are not there because they have an expectation of a high wage. They are there because they love to work with children despite the wages. We believe that assertion skills will help manage some of the stressful situations so that the job can be more controllable and rewarding.

Imposter syndrome

Imposter syndrome is something that has been discussed as an attribute of successful women. It is a feeling of not deserving the success that they have and a worry that one-day 'someone' will discover that they are not worthy of the position and status that they have and will strip them of it. Clance and Imes (1978) discuss how this is a syndrome that is found in women and that men do not have these same feelings. They discuss at length the reasons for this syndrome and pinpoint that women who are successful worry that their achievements somehow affect their perception of their femininity.

Clance and Imes note that according to Mead, a woman's femininity is called into question by her success. Martina Horner's (1972) studies support Mead's observation that for a woman to succeed in our culture is indeed a fearsome venture. Horner indicates that many women have motive to avoid success out of a fear that they will be rejected or considered less feminine if they do succeed (Clance and Imes, 1978)

It may seem that at first reading this syndrome is not applicable to women working in early years at it could be argued that this work is almost entirely staffed by women and is seen as naturally 'women's work' so how could women feel like imposters? Furthermore society bestows an approval on women working in this field, as it is an extension of the stereotypically viewed 'inherent' female qualities of nurturing, caring and parenting. A practitioner attending one of our courses on assertion, when asked what they considered to be an essential pre requisite in an early years practitioner said without hesitation 'motherhood – being a mum', and we feel that this is a popular view held both within and without the sector.

Of course we would argue, as would others, that caring and educating other people's children requires a very different skill set and knowledge base than parenting one's own children. This view is hard to maintain when every parent and carer is, naturally, an expert on his or her own child. Establishing and retaining the idea of being a specialist and having added knowledge and skills above and beyond those of the parent/carer is a hard task. This is especially true when the practitioner's goal is to work in partnership with parents and respect their knowledge and relationship with their child.

Moreover, working with team members, other childcare professionals and managing and leading teams needs a level of transferable work based skills that equal any that are used in a range of other professional fields.

How imposter syndrome manifests itself in this work is by a feeling of 'I'm just looking after children and this is something that any woman could do'. Through our experience of teaching and training practitioners who have returned to academic learning and have achieved honours degrees and professional equivalent teaching qualifications we have often heard them minimising their achievements by attributing them to the rest of their team 'It's not just me, it's all of us' or seeing their work as lesser 'Well, I'm just a mum who needed some part time work'.

This feeling is enhanced and reinforced by the way that both society and their academic peers view their work. This doesn't just affect practitioners. We have attended meetings where lecturing in early years degrees is somehow seen as lesser than lecturing in degrees in other fields, even though the same academic rigour and university wide levels apply to all programmes.

Where are assertion skills needed?

We would say that the main areas of early years work that benefit from assertion skills are when managing staff and also having difficult conversations with parents. Additional areas would include communicating with other childcare professionals; for example social workers, OFSTED, school personnel and also training agencies and higher education institutions.

In our experience though it doesn't stop there. The feedback from practitioners who have attended our assertion workshops is that assertion skills are also useful in their personal lives. We have had anecdotal evidence that the assertion techniques that we teach have been invaluable in a range of situations from dealing with teenage traumas to taking goods back to a shop or complaining about poor service in a restaurant.

The added benefit of assertion techniques is that, once grasped, and once the practitioner sees the positive way that they can deliver difficult conversations and the way that this can be received then practice can be changed. Because these conversations can be delivered successfully with both participants having a win–win experience then relationships can be improved and the general level of communication and trust in a setting can be enhanced.

It has to be added that underpinning all of this good practice is the ultimate aim to improve the quality of experience for the children who attend the setting. Children look to the adults around them for examples of behaviours to adopt, as they grow older. We are all familiar with the way that children re-enact situations that they have seen adults take part in, for example in the role-play area or with the small world equipment. In the same way children need to see the adults around them interacting with each other in a respectful assertive way. Adults then becomes positive role models for children and an example of how people should deal with each other – in an honest, congruent way. A way in which both praise and critical feedback can be given and received through open channels of communication. By this we mean that the setting has an ethos of trust and respect for each other's professionalism. Assertion skills will feed into and bolster this ethos and provide a happier and more focused workplace.

References

Baker, R. (2012) '"Childcare is not just a woman's job" – why only two per cent of the day nurseries and childcare workforce is male' available at http://www.daynurseries.co.uk/news/article.cfm/id/1557858/childcare-is-not-just-a-womans-job-why-only-two-per-cent-of-the-day-nurseries-and-childcare-workforce-is-male (accessed 11 January 2015).

Clance, P. R., and Imes, S. (1978) 'The imposter phenomenon in high achieving women: dynamics and therapeutic intervention' available at http://www.paulineroseclance.com/pdf/ip_high_achieving_women.pdf (accessed 13 April 2015).

Department for Education (2011), 'The early years foundation stage (EYFS) review' available at https://www.gov.uk/government/uploads/system/uploads/attachment_data/file/184839/DFE-00178-2011.pdf (accessed 13 April 2015).

Department for Education (2013), 'More great childcare – raising quality and giving parents more choice', available at https://www.gov.uk/government/uploads/system/uploads/attachment_data/file/219660/More_20Great_20Childcare_20v2.pdf (accessed 13 April 2015).

Horner, M. S. (1972). Toward an understanding of achievement-related conflicts in women. *Journal of Social Issues* 28(2), 157–175.Office for National Statistics (2013), 'Annual survey of hours and earnings, 2013 provisional results' available at http://www.ons.gov.uk/ons/rel/ashe/annual-survey-of-hours-and-earnings/2013-provisional-results/stb-ashe-statistical-bulletin-2013.html (accessed 13 April 2015).

Chapter 2

What is assertiveness?

Introduction

This chapter considers what assertiveness is within the broader context of communication and constructive, productive conflict in teams. We will start by acknowledging the two key cornerstones of communication and constructive conflict for effective teams and then explore a range of communication styles around conflict, of which assertiveness is just one strand. By comparing assertiveness with passive, aggressive and passive aggressive communication, we will set out the fabric and structure of assertiveness.

Early years settings and teams, like any organisation, benefit from a clear, shared vision. When a team knows and owns their vision they use this to establish meaningful goals and identify how they are going to get there. Not having a clear vision can severely limit the motivation, focus and achievements of an early years team (Price and Ota, 2014). For the purposes of this book we are going to assume that a vision is in place and focus instead on how early years teams can move more effectively towards that vision.

Working together as a team can be difficult and challenging. There are two key reasons for this; firstly, we fail to appreciate the complexity of skills, awareness and understanding needed to collaborate and cooperate together. Secondly, no one taught us how to do it. We believe that alongside a clear vision, effective teams and successful organisations are rooted in relational intelligence. This is more than just being able to do something, the skills of working together as a team. It also includes the awareness and understanding of how to connect, communicate, respect and sustain relationships in a team. Where team members share higher levels of relational intelligence they are happier, communicate effectively with each other and can achieve more (Ota, 2014).

As a starting point for determining what assertiveness is, let's pick up on two keywords, 'communicate' and 'happier'. These words are great starting points for understanding and appreciating the importance of assertiveness within an early years team.

Communication skills

'So what do you see as the two key ingredients for your team to work effectively together?'

'What kind of things do effective early years teams do? What might you hear them say? How do they feel?'

These are questions we often ask to encourage practitioners to reflect on what an effective team is and how they could further develop and improve as a team themselves. Unsurprisingly communication comes up time and time again as a fundamental cornerstone for any team to work together. Of course, communication is a good answer, without communication any team is going to flounder and struggle. However once communication is identified, it is also something we frequently delve deeper into and challenge. Communication is a huge word that covers an enormous range of different skills and elements. Even breaking it down to speaking and listening doesn't really take it much further, as both of these have their own layers of complexity and matrix of skills, awareness, understanding and vocabulary.

We'll explore this in more detail later in Chapters 7, 8 and 9. In a broad sense though, we can define communication, effective communication, as an exchange of messages between two people. Those messages are either; trying to understand someone else or getting them to understand you. Whether you are the one doing the talking or listening, both parties are necessary for the messages to be given and received. This is because both verbal and nonverbal communication is integral to what messages are exchanged and understood.

So, the case for communication as an essential part of effective teams makeup cannot be disputed. What is more helpful is to dig deeper into how we understand what communication is and how different kinds of communication styles can enable or limit a team being able to work together.

Effective teams are happier

Well, yes and no. Clearly it is reasonable to expect that successful, effective teams would be more motivated, energised and well, happy. This is in stark contrast to when teams aren't working well together and the signals are less appealing – lack of focus, low energy, stagnant and dispirited. The note of caution here is to expect or presume that effective teams should be happy all the time. Great teams are not happy all the time and that is because conflict, challenge and disagreeing with each other is another a vital ingredient alongside our broader umbrella of communication.

Assertiveness combines the two key ingredients of communication and conflict. As we discussed when looking at communication above, these are big words and in deepening our understanding of what assertiveness is, as well as how to use it in early years practice, we will delve deeper into what they are as they will help us also appreciate the features and components of assertiveness.

The importance of constructive conflict

Distinguishing between constructive and destructive conflict

Productive, or constructive conflict is necessary for teams to grow and move forwards together. It is important at the outset to be clear about the type of conflict we are advocating and distinguish constructive conflict from destructive conflict and interpersonal fighting. Personal attacks, mean spiritedness and gossiping behind people's backs (rather than face to face with the person concerned) all fall into the category of destructive conflict and do not benefit a team, the individuals in it, or the organization.

Like destructive conflict, constructive conflict can still feature passion, frustration and emotion (Lencioni, 2002, p. 202), however, there is a crucial difference as the debate, discussion and resolution of issues is ideological, not personal. This is where we revisit the importance of vision once more; constructive conflict is about discerning whether a team and organization are moving closer or further away from realising their vision. Whilst there might be heated debates and discussion those involved in constructive conflict 'emerge . . . with no residual feelings or collateral damage, but an eagerness readiness to take on the next important issue' (Lencioni, 2002, p. 203).

So constructive, productive conflict is important and necessary, it matters. Healthy conflict also saves time as team members can share how they feel, what they think, agree a way forward - and then move on. This is instead of the ongoing loop of revisiting issues that remain unexplored and unresolved.

No conflict?

We return to the somewhat mistaken notion of great teams being happy – all the time. 'We never argue and get on really well' is a worrying tell-tale sign that conflict is not being express helpfully or productively in a setting. Positive, professional relationships across an early years team does not preclude disagreeing with each other, sometimes passionately so.

Two key reasons can be identified for why this constructive conflict is often not evident in early years settings:

(1) conflict is avoided
(2) conflict is discouraged.

Conflict avoided

In our experience most early years practitioners don't like conflict and will avoid it where and when they can, opting instead for a 'quiet life'. If we probe deeper into why this might be we need to trace back into our and personal histories: a big piece of how we feel about conflict and deal with it stems from our own backgrounds and experiences as children. How was conflict expressed and allowed when we were growing up? What did we see and hear? Were there rows, quickly dealt with and done with? Or simmering, under the surface anger never really expressed or mentioned? As Lencioni (2005) explains, these personal histories often hold important clues to why we feel like we do about conflict and how we approach it as adults.

This situation can be further compounded by the image of a caring, nurturing early years practitioner. For many this identity doesn't sit easily or comfortably with conflict where the general expectations of society often perpetuate the notion that women should 'keep the peace' and 'not rock the boat'.

Addressing conflict is often a difficult conversation and for lots of reasons, as we identified in chapter 1, early years teams are frequently among the most reluctant to tackle and engage in them. When encouraged to reflect on why they might be avoiding conflict fear is frequently cited by early years colleagues. This includes fear of:

- upsetting the other person
- the person getting angry
- the person thinking I don't like them
- not being sure of the other person's reaction

- not really achieving anything
- the other person talking about me with other people
- making the situation worse.

Faced with this scenario it is easy to see how practitioners prefer to avoid the hassle and simply not address anyone or anything that could cause conflict.

Conflict discouraged

Discomfort and unease with conflict can of course extend to those with leading and management responsibilities. Leaders of teams have an important role in encouraging and providing the environment for conflict to be expressed and accepted as part of the team working together and moving forwards. Where leaders may themselves be reluctant to engage with conflict, and do not model or give permission for conflict, it is unlikely that the rest of the team will be willing or able to take the perceived risk of expressing disagreement or alternative views and opinions.

We will return in later chapters to consider the role of leaders and managers in teams for facilitating and enabling constructive conflict, for the moment it is simply for recognising that lack of expressed conflict in a team can be as much about conflict being discouraged as well is avoided.

Conflict (safely) out in the open – a place for assertiveness

The case for conflict, the right kind, has been made. We have also explored where and why conflict might remain hidden and unexpressed in early years settings and teams. Despite the hopes of many conflict avoiders, this doesn't mean that the conflict, or the issues/situation giving rise to the conflict and requiring resolution, will quietly disappear, mend or go away of its own accord.

There will always be consequences for conflict left unaddressed and unresolved and we will explore these in further chapters. Part of being an early years professional and an early as professional within a team and setting is recognising one's accountability as well as the accountability of others; it is taking responsibility for oneself as well as responsibility for others in your team. To achieve this effectively requires communication skills and productive conflict. Assertiveness brings together these two elements; it is an effective communication tool to address and resolve conflict.

Locating assertiveness within different kinds of communication

When people find themselves in a situation that they do not like, for whatever reason, they can communicate with those around them in different ways. Assertiveness is just one communication style that people use and it is best understood when located within the spectrum of passive and passive aggressive to aggressive styles and behaviours. Each style of communication incorporates its own way of talking, its own aims and outcomes and impact, both for the person talking and those around them receiving the message.

The differences between passive, aggressive and assertive communication will be expanded and illustrated in more detail in Chapter 3. To unpick the nature of assertiveness communication, let us compare either end of the spectrum: passive and aggressive communication.

Their differences are summarised in the Table 2.1:

Table 2.1 A summary of passive aggressive communication.

	Passive	Aggressive
What is said	Saying too little – hard to sustain because it's like you've swallowed something and it can come out inappropriately. Not expressing your rights, feelings, opinions and needs.	Saying too much – hard to sustain because it's draining in exhausting. Expressing your own rights, feelings, needs and opinions with no respect for the rights and feelings of others. Often expressing feelings in a demanding and angry way.
How do you see yourself?	Not worth much. Having little to contribute.	My needs and opinions more important than others.
How do you see others?	More important than me.	Having little to contribute.
Aims	To avoid conflict at all times and please others.	To win, ignoring the feelings of others.
Impact short term	Reduction of anxiety and avoid guilt.	May seem rewarding, e.g. release of tension and sense of power.
Impact longer term	Continuing loss of self-esteem. May cause others to become irritated by you and develop lack of respect.	May be less beneficial e.g. feeling guilty, resentment of people around you. May cause problems for you and those around you.

Assertiveness

If passive and aggressive communication are at either end of a spectrum, assertiveness sits in the middle within these two styles. Where a passive approach can be characterised by, 'I lose you win' and an aggressive approach by, 'I win, you lose', then assertiveness is about creating a win-win situation. Assertiveness is about expressing your own rights, feelings, needs and opinions whilst at the same time maintaining respect for the other person's own rights, feelings, needs and opinions. Assertive communication takes a more solution focused approach and is a way of taking responsibility for oneself and expressing feelings in a direct, honest and appropriate way. Being assertive doesn't always mean that you will get your own way, or that she will always 'win'. However, it does mean that you will be able to walk away from any situation knowing that you have expressed yourself and put across what you wanted to say.

We will take a step-by-step approach to examining assertive communication in Chapter 3, but before moving on, a word about passive aggressive communication styles.

Passive aggressive communication styles

Passive aggressive behaviour and communication is more subtle and can be harder to pin down. Fundamentally the person using this is aiming to disguise how they truly feel and there is usually a huge mismatch between what the person says and what their body language or tone of voice is communicating. As with passive communication, anger and frustration is not expressed but is instead bottled up and repressed as a quietly brewing resentment. Hostility is indirectly communicated through negative behaviour and can include anything from passive resistance to every day tasks to stubbornness, willful incompetence, resentment and contradictory behaviour (Dvorsky, 2015). The 'passive' part of passive aggressive should not be a distraction as it can be more destructive than aggression on its own.

Passive aggressive communication can make be very difficult for others to identify, engage with and respond to and colleagues who rely on passive aggressive kinds of communication can be difficult to interact with and relate to. Passive aggressive colleagues may be recognised in those who:

- feel underappreciated
- lack accountability and place the blame on others

- procrastinates or misses deadlines when they don't agree with the task
- appear grumpy or irritable but won't say why
- use notes or emails to communicate in difficult situations.

So where does this communication style and behaviour come from? To understand where this kind of communication style comes from we can refer, once again, back to the importance of our childhood experiences of conflict, as well as the aforementioned issue of gender conditioning and stereotyping around discouraging the expressing of conflict. Signe Whitson (Dvorsky, 2015) also provides further possible reasons:

(1) Anger is socially unacceptable.
(2) Sugarcoated hostility is socially acceptable.
(3) Passive aggression is easier than assertiveness, and a sign of immaturity.
(4) Passive aggression is easily rationalised.
(5) Revenge is sweet: 'Because it can be difficult to "catch in the act" and often impossible to discipline according to standard HR protocols, passive aggressive behaviour often exists as the perfect office crime'.
(6) Passive aggressive behaviour is convenient, allows one to avoid an actual fight.
(7) Passive aggressive behaviour can be powerful, allowing the perpetrator to channel their own anger and frustrations through the reactions of their target.

Clearly passive aggressive communication does not enable constructive conflict in teams and early years settings. We will continue to explore passive aggressive communication and ways to address this in later chapters.

Back to assertiveness

Teams and the individuals in them need the right kind of conflict, which in turn requires a particular kind of communication. Assertiveness is the kind of communication that can ground conflict as a constructive and important part of how a team works together and moves closer to its vision. Assertive communication and the three-step approach we propose in this book (see Chapter 3) is an effective communication tool for improving our own communication and responding respectfully and effectively to different kinds of passive, aggressive and passive aggressive communication in others.

Having outlined the main elements of assertiveness, in contrast to other means of communicating, we will turn to look more closely at how assertive communication sounds and is structured.

References

Council Directory (2015) 'Passive aggressive behaviour', available at http://www. counselling-directory.org.uk/passive-aggressive.html (accessed 2 May 2015).

Dvorsky, G. (2015) 'The secrets to handling passive–aggressive people', available at http://io9.com/the-secrets-to-handling-passive-aggressive-people-1681127156 (accessed 2 May 2015).

Lencioni, P. (2002) *The five dysfunctions of a team*, San Francisco: Jossey-Bass.

Lencioni, P. (2005) *Overcoming the five dysfunctions of a team – a field guide*, San Francisco: Jossey-Bass.

Ota, C. (2014) 'Relational intelligence', available at http://cathyota.com/relational-intelligence (accessed 2 May 2015).

Price, D., and Ota, C. (2014) *Leading and supporting early years teams*, Oxford: Routledge.

Chapter 3

The structure of assertiveness communication – how to do it

Assertiveness is like a muscle that needs to be flexed, worked and regularly used in order to become strong. In becoming assertive we may become discouraged by the reactions of people around us. If we have usually responded to situations in a passive way then our friends, family and colleagues can misinterpret our assertiveness as aggression. The ways that we are acting are so different to our usual responses that others can become alarmed and worried and want us to change back into our usual passive demeanor.

We would advise the practitioner to continue working the assertion muscle and train the people around them to see you in a new light, as someone who is confidant and able to voice their feelings and talk clearly about the actions that they want to happen in the future.

We detail the three-point plan for assertive behaviour below. We would advise that when using this plan it is useful to try it out in a situation where the outcome is not so loaded or emotionally charged as when using it at home or work. It is ideal for complaining about poor service or goods and especially where the outcome is not significant for you.

Read the case study below and think about the relevance for yourself. Can you recognise any elements of your own behaviour in these different responses?

Case study 3.1

Lindsay is in a café with her three friends looking forward to her birthday lunch. She has been in this café many times before and is confidant that they are going to have a nice time. They give their order for food and drink to the waitress. The drinks arrive quickly and the group starts catching up and chatting to each other. After 30 minutes they start looking around for their meal and they see some food on the counter and the waiting staff are talking together by the cash desk and ignoring the food. Eventually one of the staff goes over to the food and slowly brings it to the table, puts it in front of them and leaves quickly. When they start to eat the food they realise that it's cold.

Possible scenarios

One

Lindsay gets out of her chair and marches over to the first member of staff she can find. This is not the person who took her order or the one who delivered it but she doesn't care because she is so angry. The conversation takes place in the middle of the restaurant with the whole place looking on.

Lindsay:	'This is totally unacceptable'.
Waiter (looking bemused):	'What is? I've only just started my shift'.
Lindsay:	'Get the manager right now – no, don't bother because we're leaving'.
Waiter:	'Shall I get you your bill?'
Lindsay:	'You've got a nerve, we're not paying for a thing'.

While Lindsay and her party get their coats on the manager is summoned and Lindsay starts shouting at them. The manager in turn starts threatening to call the police because of the unpaid drinks bill. The whole party makes an undignified exit and know that they can never visit that café, or indeed walk past it again. The birthday lunch is not a success and Lindsay's initial euphoria at having given the waiter a piece of her mind wears off and she is left feeling miserable and depressed.

Two

Lindsay starts to eat the lukewarm food and, as it's her birthday and as the other friends are taking her lead, they do too. The food is unpleasant and the conversation is stilted. Sensing the awkwardness the manager comes over and asks them if everything is OK with their order. Lindsay says 'yes' through gritted teeth and the rest of the party stay silent. The meal finishes quickly and the bill is paid. Everyone goes his or her separate ways and the lunch is not a success.

When Lindsay gets home her daughter asks her 'Everything OK mum, did you have a nice time?'

'No I did not' Lindsay snaps 'and it isn't helped by knowing what a state your room is in, go upstairs and sort it out right now'. Her daughter goes up in tears shouting 'I wish I hadn't made you a birthday card after all'. So not only is Lindsay's lunch ruined but her evening is miserable as well.

Three

Lindsay attracts the attention of the waiter who took their original order. She walks with him to the quiet area where the till is. 'The food has arrived late and it's cold' she starts 'I am very disappointed as I've been here before and always liked it.' She continues and ends with 'We are willing to pay for the drinks that we have but I am not paying for the food'.

The waiter says 'Sorry about that, I'll just get the manager'. The manager arrives and says 'I understand you are upset, but it is our policy that you have to pay for the food you have ordered'.

Lindsay replies, 'I am not upset, I am disappointed. As I said I think it's reasonable to pay for the drinks but not food that I didn't eat and that was cold and late. I have always had good lunches here and I use this café a lot'.

'OK' says the manager 'I accept that we have had some staffing problems here today and it is only because of that I will make an exception to our policy and take the cost of the food off your bill'.

'I appreciate that' says Lindsay 'Hopefully this won't happen again when I next come in – I am sure that it is a one off as you say'.

First step

Do you notice the initial conversation that Lindsay had with the waiter in option three? She started the exchange by being very clear about what had happened. *'The food has arrived late and it's cold'*. This means that the waiter and Lindsay have a clear outline of what they will now be discussing. The agenda is firmly on the table and both parties are aware of what it is. This is a different possibility to one where she just says 'This is unacceptable' to a random member of staff. Lindsay has also made an effort to find someone who will know some of the background to the incident.

This is good practice in any negotiating as it makes it clear to all parties concerned what is on the table for discussion and what are the boundaries of the negotiating.

So the first step in the three-point assertion plan is to state what you are going to talk about.

Second step

Lindsay then proceeds to say something about her feelings in the incident *'I am very disappointed as I've been here before and always liked it'*. Notice that she uses 'I' statements. This is very different from saying 'You' as in 'You have made me very annoyed'. Making a 'you' statement can mean that the person thus addressed will be defensive and try to argue against the accusation 'How can I have made you annoyed? You are over reacting'. If Lindsay stays with 'I' statements then it is hard to argue or divert the exchange. The waiter is unlikely to say 'No, you aren't disappointed'. Whenever you use 'I' statements you clearly own the feelings that you are declaring and showing that you are the expert on your own feelings and so making it difficult for anyone to take offence or to deny your statement.

This might seem a strange thing to do at first – how can you have feelings about taking something back to a shop? The truth is that there will be feelings there, even if they are minor and the situation isn't an important one. Feelings of regret, annoyance, disappointment, frustration – you need to identify and name the feeling that you have. It is very unlikely that there will be no feelings at all – even if your definition of 'feeling' is usually something more profound.

The second step in the plan is to say how you are feeling using an 'I' statement.

Third step

This can be the hardest part of the three-point approach. Can you see that Lindsay states what she wants to happen in the future *'We are willing to pay for the drinks that we have but I am not paying for the food'* Lindsay is very clear about her plan. This is important because it means that she is taking control over the outcome of the exchange. In many cases the person she is talking to will be relieved as it gives them both something to negotiate about. This puts Lindsay in a strong position as she has decided and defined the outcome and the manager can only say 'yes' or 'no'. Of course it is possible that they might put a different possibility on the table 'If you pay the whole bill I will give you a voucher for 50% off on your next two visits'. This then gets Lindsay into a whole other range of negotiating possibilities where they can both bargain and compromise. For the purposes of this exchange and to make the process simpler we suggest that the manager accepts the proposal that Lindsay has outlined.

However, the manager does counter with an objection, '*I understand you are upset, but it is our policy that you have to pay for the food you have ordered*'. Lindsay skillfully manages this argument, '*I am not upset, I am disappointed. As I said I think it's reasonable to pay for the drinks but not food that I didn't eat and that was cold and late. I have always had good lunches here and I use this café a lot*'.

You can see that Lindsay begins by restating her feelings as she has had them misinterpreted by the manager. She then repeats the outcome that she wants using slightly different language and reminding the manager that she is a regular and, until now, happy customer. You might recognise this as the 'three stars and a wish'[1] type approach that primary schools sometimes use. She is tempering the request by ending on a positive note but being clear about why she is making the request by restating her original complaint.

Of course in this case study the manager capitulates, albeit in a grudging way that implies that this is a one off and that Lindsay would not have her request agreed to if it happened again. Lindsay expresses her approval of this end to the negotiations and her closing statement reminds the manager that she is a regular customer and that this incident should only be a one off – as they have said.

The last step in the three-point plan is to say what you want to happen in the future.

Outcomes

We hope that it is clear in the first two scenarios that the outcomes of both are not satisfactory. In the first one Lindsay has reacted in an aggressive way and, although the drama and emotion of the moment carries her through, this leaves her feeling dispirited and low. She relives the incident in her mind and possibly regrets her outburst.

Even if she doesn't, she knows that she cannot revisit the café and when she meets her friends again one of them confides that Lindsay's row was embarrassing for her and that she thought that Lindsay should be careful of 'seeing red' as it isn't the first time it has happened. She adds that the whole café was looking at them and did Lindsey notice that the manager of a local clothes shop that they all go to was sitting on another table?

In the second scenario there is no drama in the restaurant as no one complains or says anything. As a result Lindsey feels upset and frustrated at herself and takes these feelings out at someone familiar. If we are passive the feelings of frustration with the inner monologue of 'Why didn't I say that' and 'what if I had done this' can build up. We may not have acted the way we would have liked to because of reserve and feelings of shame and embarrassment. These can be linked to gender and also be culturally specific. When we return to a familiar environment like the home the load becomes too much and we can snap and lose out temper with those nearest to us as we have no such reservations about our behaviour with them.

When she next meets up with her friends they joke about Lindsay being a 'doormat' and she joins in the laughter but secretly feels ashamed.

In the third possible scenario Lindsay follows the three-point plan and of course everything turns out well! Our point is that, even if Lindsey hadn't achieved her aim she would have left the incident feeling that she had behaved with dignity and, as an adult should. The plan doesn't mean that the other person or people involved have to agree to your demands. The manager could have forced Lindsay to pay for the meal. Lindsey could have used the 'broken record' technique. To use the broken record method, simply repeat what you want in a calm, collected manner, offering no explanations or rationalizations (Smith 2003).

In this scenario, with a little effort, Lindsay can leave knowing that she has been clear in her behaviour. What is also important is that the manager has not been humiliated but has felt able to admit that there is a problem and has had that recognised and validated by Lindsay. She has not replied 'Well, that's not my concern, you should manage your staff better' and set up a feeling of defensiveness when they admit that there is a problem. Her assertive stance has made it possible for the manager to be honest.

The group leaves the café and still has time to go somewhere else and have a slightly shorter lunch. They joke with Lindsay while they eat their sandwiches in the next café and say that she should get a job with the United Nations!

It's interesting to now transfer this to a work situation in an early years setting to see how the same skills and technique can be applied where the outcome is much more crucial in terms of professional development.

Case study 3.2

Louise is a room leader in a private day nursery. The shifts have recently changed and she is on an early 8am start with a younger and less experienced colleague, Becky. Since the change in starting time Becky has been late every day. Louise has had to set up the room herself and then Becky has been coming in just before the children arrive – she has apologised every time and has then not mentioned it again or offered an explanation as to why she is late.

Possible scenarios

Aggressive behaviour

Louise lets this situation carry on for four days, she is seething and makes sarcastic remarks every day 'Oh you decided to join us did you?' She spends the days ignoring Becky pointedly and glaring at her when she has to talk to her. On the last day she blows up at Becky as she sets foot in the door. 'How dare you come in late again, you really are a waste of space aren't you, probably spending too long on your makeup and hair in the morning?' Becky bursts into tears and runs to the staff toilet where she locks herself in and refuses to come out. The children and parents start to arrive and Louise has to deal with this on her own, she is flustered and red faced and feeling very under pressure. The parents sense that something is awry and look at each other and Louise. The children also pick up on the feeling of conflict and ask where Becky is. There is a sense of anxiety in the room and children are fretful and difficult to settle into the day's routine. The manager comes into the room on her daily rounds and immediately springs into action, she allocates two other staff to the room and persuades Becky out of the toilet and into another room. She talks to Louise in the office and tells her that she should have let her know about the situation and that it was unprofessional to shout at Becky in the way that she did.

Louise feels very hard done by as she feels that none of this is her fault and that Becky has managed to avoid any censure for her actions. In the long term this episode makes for an uncomfortable schism in the staff team as Louise tries to make other staff members choose sides between her and Becky and avoids talking to Becky. Becky is happy in her new room and Louise feels jealousy and resentment that stops her enjoying her job.

DISCUSSION

Can you see that Louise's actions are on the aggressive end of the assertive scale with some passive aggressive behaviour mixed in there as well? She is behaving in a passive aggressive manner at first as she does not confront Becky directly with her grievance but makes sarcastic remarks and uses negative body language instead of direct communication.

Because she has not expressed herself directly Louise feels frustrated and eventually reaches 'boiling point' and reacts with anger to Becky. This has wide reaching effects, not just with Becky but also with the children, parents and other staff and managers of the setting.

Passive behaviour

The same situation is happening with Louise and Becky. In this version of the scenario Louise does not confront Becky. Instead she sighs and obviously starts moving equipment and resources when Becky arrives. Becky tries to help her but Louise pushes her offer away 'No you go and get your coat off, I'm fine.' She smiles at Becky but it is through gritted teeth.

Again, when the children and parents arrive they sense that there is an 'atmosphere' and the nursery room is not a happy place as Becky works silently and Louise seethes quietly. Louise does not talk to the manager about the situation, instead the gossips to the other members of staff about Becky and makes disparaging remarks about her practice 'I'm not being funny but I wonder how she ever got her level 3'. Becky senses that staff members have been talking about her, as Louise is often the centre of laughter in the staff room that stops suddenly when she walks in.

Louise is frustrated by the situation with Becky and is often short tempered and unhappy at home because of it. When confronted by her partner she tells them the situation but says 'I don't say anything, I wouldn't give her the satisfaction. Anyway I can do my job as well as hers as she is so useless.'

DISCUSSION

Can you see that Louise is behaving in a passive and a passive/aggressive way? She is not dealing with the situation directly and honestly. Instead she is ignoring the actual problem and concentrating on another issue – that she thinks that Becky is not a good practitioner. She is also using the passive tactic of spreading rumour and gossip rather than actually deal directly with someone. Her actions have consequences for the whole setting as they unsettle the children and families that use the setting and spread discord amongst the staff team. Her actions also have consequences for her personal life, as she is not happy at home and not able to talk honestly about her feelings of frustration. As a result, what could be a contained incident spreads ripples far beyond the importance of the initial problem and for much longer.

Assertive behaviour

The second day that Becky is late Louise greets her briskly and manages to arrange for them to both have a break later at the same time. She asks Becky to have a chat in a quiet corner and says 'Becky you were late yesterday and today. I feel very disappointed and annoyed, as I have had to do a lot of extra work to cover for you. We need to discuss why you aren't managing to get in on time and sort it out so that the rest of this week will be different.

Becky tells Louise that her mum isn't well and that she is popping by every morning to check in with her on the way to work. She didn't want to say anything as it upsets her and she wants to start work feeling happy. She knows that her mum has just had a bad virus and will be better soon but she finds it upsetting to see her so unwell.

Louise says that she is glad that Becky has told her this and she is sorry for Becky's mum. She suggests that Becky changes shifts for the rest of the week and tells her that she will arrange it with the manager if Becky feels unable to talk about it. Becky thanks her and then confides that sometimes with Louise she feels awkward because Louise has been at the nursery so much longer and is more experienced than her.

DISCUSSION

Can you see how Louise uses the three-point plan? She states what the situation is clearly, she then continues by saying how she feels about it and concludes by stating the outcome she wants to see for the future. Here I have also shown that by doing this extra facts are revealed by Becky. What is important here is that the true story of the incident is now revealed and Becky also feels supported enough to tell Louise something that she is thinking and an area of vulnerability – she is pushing the Johari's window that we mention in chapter seven. By doing this she is establishing trust between the two practitioners and establishing a relationship that is based on honesty.

Louise in her turn is able to act professionally and support Becky while still having her demands met. The situation is resolved speedily and efficiently with no loss of status or humiliation to either people concerned. Louise is acting as a manager of the room and a support to a younger, less experienced member of staff. Because Becky confided in her she does not gossip about her in the staff room. Becky feels supported and is able to tell a few other staff members about her mum's illness and this results in concern and a feeling of inclusion for Becky that bolsters her self-esteem and improves her practice.

There is no air of conflict in the room, indeed the opposite, as Becky and Louise have a closer working relationship. The manager sees what an effective role model Louise is to Becky and resolves to extend her skills by making her the mentor for the students on placement at the nursery.

Of course this is a fabricated situation but we hope that you can see how actions have consequences and some of these can be far reaching. This is true generally but even more so in the tight knit and close community of an early years setting.

The three-point plan relies on people being honest with each other and having good communication skills. It is also supported if the ethos of the nursery is that members of the staff team are able to hold each other accountable without feeling that there is personal conflict. If these underpinning routines and ways of practice are in place it makes it more difficult for people to behave in a passive aggressive way or to spread gossip and rumour as a way of retaliation.

Other people

In these two case studies the three points plan results in a very positive outcome. Of course we realise that real life is not so contrived. It is important to remember that using these three steps does not automatically guarantee that the outcome will be the one that is desired. The only definite outcome will be that the person acting assertively will be able to leave the encounter knowing that they have acted professionally and in a congruent manner. They shouldn't feel the need to compound the incident by behaving badly either at home or in work, as they should feel that their actions, at least, have been a true reflection of how they feel.

Other people can act in an unpredictable and unforeseen way. Becky could have responded to Louise's clear statements with aggression or passive behaviour of her own. She could have shouted at Louise 'You don't understand, you're so horrible' and fled to the bathroom in tears. She could have just agreed with Louise that something needed to be done, not given any more details, and then gossiped with the rest of the staff team that Louise was unfair and coldhearted as she was horrible to her when she (Becky) was upset.

Tears are not a reason to stop an assertive episode completely. Louise could respond by acknowledging that Becky is upset and asking her if she wants a minute to contain herself and stating that it might be better to continue this conversation at the end of the day when she has had time to prepare herself. In this way she is being sympathetic to Becky's distress but also showing that the issue has not vanished.

She is not saying 'Oh don't cry and don't worry, I'll just carry on setting up the room in the mornings, I don't mind'. Neither is she saying 'Oh that's it, start with the crocodile tears, typical!' It is important in this situation to show that while you are understanding and sensitive there is also an issue that needs to be dealt with.

Place and time

In the second case study Louise was able to choose a place and time to deal with the episode. We appreciate that this is not always possible. For example, in the first case study that is set in a café the situation had to be dealt with at once. However, even then Lindsay was able to pull a waiter to one side and talk to them in an alcove away from the main diners. Her conversation with the manager was also conducted discreetly. In this way the manager didn't feel that they had to prove their superiority in front of the other people in the café, staff and customers, they could act in a way that was more honest and in tune with their real feelings.

Louise could choose a time and a place more freely and this also meant that both people were more able to talk honestly and openly without an audience that would influence their interchange. Time had passed and Louise was feeling calmer after her annoyance of the morning. Becky was also feeling less upset and worried about Louise's reaction to her lateness.

Body language and tone

Assertive body language/tone of voice – it's not just what you say but how you say it that's important. Below are some pointers to think about when delivering an assertive message.

- Face the other person, standing or sitting straight.
- Listen carefully to what they say.
- Have a pleasant facial expression.
- Keep your voice calm and pleasant.
- Make sure that your body language supports what you are saying (e.g. some people make the mistake of nodding their head when they are trying to say 'no!').

Finally

If you are using the three-point plan to deal with a difficult situation then we would recommend giving some thought to setting up a time and a place that is more receptive to open and honest exchanges. Dealing with an emotive situation while feelings of anger, annoyance, disappointment or fear of consequence are very present for everyone concerned is never an easy or efficient option. It is far better, if at all possible, to try and get at least the time or the place, and ideally both, ready for an honest and professional discussion. We refer to this again in Chapter 4.

Note

1 This is often used by teachers when marking children's work. It stands for 'three things you have done very well and one thing to think about next time'.

Reference

Smith, M. (2003) 'When I say no I feel guilty', available at http://www.transcendedu.com/upload/when-i-say-no-i-feel-guilty-smith-e.pdf (accessed 15 September 2014).

Part 2

Using it

Chapter 4

Assertiveness for the early years practitioner

In this chapter we will be looking at the early years practitioner and the most effective way that they can use assertion skills. We are using this model as the base model and thinking that for all practitioners it is relevant to think about day-to-day interactions with parents and with colleagues as a starting point. Later on in the book we think about the 'bolt on' roles that practitioners may take on: a room leader, a manager, a supervisor. Our aim is that by the end of the book we have covered through the range of case studies most of the scenarios where assertion skills might be needed. Practitioners can adapt these scenarios to fit situations where they have had to have difficult conversations, deal with mis communication, repair a fractured relationship, try and assert their own professional values and instill trust and show a positive role model of doing this to children.

We have spoken elsewhere in the book about the tension between early years practitioners as professionals and also as deliverers of a service that parents buy into. Private and voluntary settings are small businesses and are, as such, vulnerable to market forces and also engaged in marketing and promotion of their services.

Working with children is a professional role and, as practitioners are aware, requires training, experience and a commitment to making a difference in children's lives. The issue to note is that it is not the same role as parenting. Many more people are parents than are early years practitioners. Because the two roles can be confused practitioner's skills and experience isn't always valued as much as it should be.

People outside the early years workforce can see the job as being a form of parenting and so something comes 'naturally' to the mainly female workforce. If people wanted advice on their financial matters, a legal issue, a technical problem with their computer or their house then they would consult a professionally trained person. They would accept that this package of information was something that they did not have expertise in themselves and defer to another's knowledge.

Because the same respect isn't always given to the skills and experience that early years workers have they are not consulted in the same way. In parenting everyone believes that they are an expert and that the way that they parent is the correct way. Small discusses how parenting is a social process and not just the actions of an individual (Small, 1998). How we parent is influenced by our individual experiences of being parented and in a wider sphere by cultural and societal values.

The relationship between parent and practitioner is crucial to the well-being and experience of the child in a day care setting. It forms part of one of the four guiding principles that the most recent review of the EYFS is built on: 'Children learn and develop well in enabling environments, in which their experiences respond to their individual needs and there is a strong partnership between practitioners and parents and/or carers' (Department for Education, 2004, p. 6). The relationship is therefore essential and can be fraught with difficulties and underpinned by issues around the perceived status of the practitioner, the feelings that the parent has about leaving a child in day care, the feelings that the practitioner has about the same issue, the ideas that they have about crucial decisions such as sleeping patterns, feeding, toileting and learning.

This relationship is based on respectful communication and the recognition of each other's important role in the child's life. Many things can upset this delicate relationship. For example, when a parent's ideas about crucial childcare practices challenge those that the practitioner has learnt in their studies. The practitioner needs to respect the parent's viewpoint and right to parent the child in the way that they wish to while also giving the parent the new information from their own bank of skills and experience.

From another perspective – the practitioner may have feelings about the parent who leaves a baby in daycare from 8am – 6pm five days a week so that they can return to their work role. It maybe that the practitioner has chosen to work in early years because it fitted in with their own childcare commitments. These opposing views are both common scenarios that we have come across in our work with practitioners.

The case study that this chapter discusses is based on this idea of different perspectives on what are the basis for respectful and healthy interactions between parents and practitioners and an analysis of it should be valuable for all practitioners as it lays the framework for this good communication.

Case study

Pearl works in a toddler room in a full-time day care nursery. The children are all two to three years old. Pearl has recently completed a foundation degree in early years care and education and she is a key worker for a group of four children. In line with the settings guidelines on parent and practitioner partnerships Pearl's room leader – Jo – has set up times when the key workers can meet up individually with parents to talk through their child's care and education. The setting also sends out regular news-letters and has an open door policy where parents can come in and sit in on any sessions. In addition the toddler room maintains communication books that go between parents and practitioners.

Pearl feels that she has a good relationship with the parents of the four children that she is especially responsible for. She is younger than any of them and they are all experienced parents who have had experience of at least one other child attending the setting.

Last week the parents of one of the children, Molly, came into the set-ting a bit early and sat in the book corner looking through books as Molly finished an art activity with Pearl. Molly was happy to stay with Pearl and was aware of her mother. Pearl was also aware of Molly's mother but tried not to alter her actions in any way. The next day Molly's mother – Lucy – came in to drop Pearl at the setting and then asked if she could 'have a word' with Pearl. Pearl checked with Jo and was able to leave the toddler room and take Lucy into the office. Pearl was nervous as she hadn't had much to do with Lucy as it was Molly's other mother who generally dropped off and picked Molly up and also came to the one to one two months ago when there seemed to be no problems.

Molly seemed nervous as well, she was flushed and while she was talk-ing she didn't look Pearl in the eye but kept looking at Molly's coat that she held in her hands and was fiddling with.

'I was listening to you talking to Molly yesterday' Lucy started 'and I felt that you talked to her as though she was older than she actually is'. Lucy went on to say that she and Molly's other mother wanted to make sure that Molly 'stayed a child' and that she was their baby and their last child and they didn't want her to 'grow up before her time'.

'I know that you have all of these qualifications' Lucy continued 'but we just want someone to play with Molly and make sure that she's safe – she's not your experiment to try all of your new ideas out on'.

Pearl didn't know what to say, she could feel that she was becoming tearful and muttered something about talking to Jo and getting back to Lucy and being very sorry. She ushered Lucy out of the office and the setting on the pretext that there was another meeting she had to go to. When she got back to the toddler room Jo could see that there was something wrong but Pearl couldn't talk to her and took herself into the toilet so that she could cry.

Possible responses

Think about what Pearl could have said to Lucy if she hadn't been so overwhelmed by her feelings. Some examples, could be:

'I don't see Molly as an experiment, I feel insulted that you would think that and I need you to understand that I am a professional early years worker and I deliver the best possible care to Molly'.

'I understand that you think I'm talking to Molly in too grown up a way, I feel unsure how to change this. What would help me is if you gave me some examples'.

'I can hear that you want Molly to enjoy her childhood; I also feel that this is so important. I would find it hard to change the way I just spoke to Molly but I hope that you can trust me that I will do everything I can to make sure that she has lots of opportunities to play and do the things she enjoys at nursery. Perhaps you could come again and see me with Molly so that you feel reassured that I am doing this?'

Reflections

We have used the three-point plan of assertiveness in each of the examples of possible responses above but we would hope that you could see that the first two contain elements of an aggressive and a passive aggressive retort.

What we would urge when reading this is to think about the desired outcome of the interaction. Pearl needs Lucy to feel confidant that Molly's needs are being met. Pearl also needs to rebuild the trust that Lucy has in the skills and experience that Pearl has. We feel that the last response acknowledges the issue that is at the bottom of Lucy's concerns. She feels that Molly shouldn't have to take on anything that is not age appropriate. In fact Pearl's training would mean that she feels the same way. Pearl can show that they have this as a shared concern. She has to let Lucy know that she is a professional and doesn't feel that it would be helpful to change her practice around voice tone in order to respond to Lucy's concerns – that this wouldn't actually make a difference. What she can do is make sure that Lucy can see that Pearl's actual practice with Molly does all the things that Lucy wants.

In this way Pearl is firstly reassuring Lucy that she takes her concerns seriously and is doing everything she can to work in partnership with her. Importantly she is also standing her ground in terms of her tone of voice and her professional judgment.

When working with early years teams who are experiencing difficulties we always recommend starting by looking at shared common agreement. An example of this would be 'We all want the best possible experience for the children who come to this setting'. Once we establish a culture of agreement it is easier to move on incrementally to find other things that the team agrees on and to discuss professionally where they don't agree. Usually they agree on the fundamental principles but disagree on how best to put them into practice.

The same idea can be applied to this interaction. Pearl and Lucy agree that they want the best professional education and care for Molly. Where they disagree is that the language and tone that Pearl uses is not age appropriate. What Pearl is offering Lucy is a chance to be reassured that Pearl can still adhere to the fundamental tenant that they agree on. If Lucy is reassured that this is being met then she may be able to see Pearl's delivery of it as part of Pearl's professionalism and individual way of practice and not as a threat to the values that she holds dear.

We can see that the first statement is aggressive and challenging. However the second statement – by asking for proof – is also challenging in an indirect way. There are times when it is right to challenge, we are not saying that this should never happen, see our comments on constructive conflict. In this case the challenge will not support the main outcome that Pearl wants, to repair the damaged relationship between herself and Lucy.

Pearl has no intention of changing her tone or way of speaking with Molly. She feels strongly that it is part of her own practice not to have a different tone when speaking to children and she thinks that this shows respect for them and her experience is that they respond well to it. To infer to Lucy that she will change if Lucy gives her some examples is not congruent and if she tries to argue with Lucy about specific examples and if they show an adult tone two things may happen. Firstly, she will further damage the trust that Lucy has with her practice and secondly she will be ignoring the underpinning point that Lucy is making about age appropriate experiences. Pearl would be making the whole disagreement about adult-to-adult interaction rather than what it actually is about which is the best way to meet the needs of the child.

Jo

We also need to consider Jo's role in this. Jo is the room leader and needs to be involved in this disagreement and how Pearl has handled it. In the first scenario where Pearl is upset it is likely that Jo will get involved at a much earlier stage, as Pearl has not been able to respond well.

Time and place

One of the important points we make in this book is about time and place in relation to being assertive. It might be that at that moment Pearl was not able to come out with an appropriate response. She was upset and unprepared. That is the reality of the situation and we would not want any practitioner to feel that they had failed just because they hadn't been able to act in an assertive and appropriate way in that instant. The main issue in that case is to show this and suggest a follow up time.

'I need to think about your comments in more depth. Would it be OK if I gave you a call at the end of today or tomorrow morning and we could have another talk? I want to make sure that I think this through properly'.

Pearl could then go to Jo and talk through a plan of action and perhaps rehearse what she wants to say and offer to Lucy as a response. Jo's role here is to support Pearl to follow through herself. If Jo is left with Pearl feeling upset and a possible complaint from a parent she may feel that she has to take total control of the situation. She may feel a range of things: That she needs to protect Pearl from further upset, that she needs to head off a complaint from a parent that may bypass her and go to the manager – this would reflect badly on her practice, that she needs to step in as Pearl is not equipped to.

If Pearl is able to give Lucy a holding statement and get some coaching from Jo then the best outcome is for her, as Molly's key person, to deal with the situation. Pearl could refer to Jo when talking to Lucy so that Lucy is aware that Jo knows about the difficulty. By letting Pearl go forward with this Jo is giving Lucy the message that she trusts Pearl's judgment and this reinforces Pearl's professionalism. Lucy does need to know that Jo is involved so that she has an understanding of how closely the practitioners work as a team.

The manager's involvement

Jo also needs to let the nursery manager know about this incident, hopefully as information rather than action needed. The manager taking action here would undermine both Jo and Pearl. Jo could have a quick word with Lucy after Pearl has dealt with the incident, perhaps referring to the, hopefully successful, outcome and perhaps mentioning that Lucy's feedback is valuable and that they might use it as a discussion point at the next team meeting with the manager. That further reinforces the team cohesion, the openness to discussing variations in practice and a willingness to take on the parent's point of view.

What would not be helpful is a knee jerk reaction from management that tells the parent that all her concerns will be addressed and certainly Pearl will alter her tone and language around Molly. This is not sustainable and also doesn't move practice on or address the real concerns that Lucy has. This reaction would be linked to the concerns we pin pointed at the beginning of this chapter about the nursery being a provider of services and the parent a buyer of these services who needs to be happy whatever the cost or issue.

Conclusion

The small business analogy above is true but there is another truth here; that the nursery is a professional registered and inspected setting staffed by trained early years practitioners. The parent must have confidence in this or they would not pay for their child to be there. Both parties have the same concerns and these need to be talked through in order to have a healthy and productive relationship. This relationship has the care and education of the child at the very core of its being – not monetary supply and demand. Exploring ways to keep practice focused on the needs of parents and children, shore up the trust in the professionalism of staff and strengthen the cooperative relationship between key workers and parents would be a productive outcome to this clash of views. In this way we hope that you can see how out of conflict a stronger and more cohesive position can be reached.

References

Department for Education, (2004) Statutory framework for the early years foundation stage, available at https://www.gov.uk/government/uploads/system/uploads/attachment_data/file/335504/EYFS_framework_from_1_September_2014__with_clarification_note.pdf (accessed 12 April 2015)

Small, M. F. (1998) *Our babies, ourselves: How biology and culture shape the way we parent*, New York: Anchor Books.

Chapter 5

Assertiveness for the early years room leader

In writing this chapter we acknowledge that there will be some overlap between this role and that of the practitioner and also the manager. In fact that is the crucial difficulty that we have pinpointed in this position and why assertion skills are so essential.

The role of the room leader involves a critical tension between being a practitioner and being a manager. The room leader is often newly promoted from practitioner status and may possibly be suddenly in a position of supervising and directing former colleagues – who may have also applied for the role.

In addition to this the room leader role will have more expectations than the practitioner role and the supervisor of the setting will need the room leader to show that they can manage a small staff team and work alongside them in a more responsible function. Parents will also liaise with the room leader as their first point of call for any issues or problems.

Analysing the role in this way we can see that of all the roles in the setting a room leader is perhaps the most demanding in terms of a variety of expectations and pressures and the one where assertion skills are most required.

The room leader is, in effect a small-scale manager, but one who is also subject to the pressures of working as a practitioner in very close proximity to colleagues. They don't have the distance of an overall manager and have to juggle the roles of supervisor, practitioner, colleague, manager with skill and dexterity.

Case study

Fran works in a large workplace nursery that is part of a nationwide chain, she has been there three years and during that time has worked in all of the rooms. She has just finished and gained a distinction in a level 3 qualification and is currently considering starting a part time BA programme and moving this forward to EYT status. She has been recently promoted as room leader of the toddler room. She has a team of three other staff members that she is responsible for. One of them, Louisa, also applied for the job but was unsuccessful. Louisa is older than Fran and has worked at the nursery for five years. She has also achieved a level 3 qualification. Her level 3 was a pass and she completed this a year ago. She is vocal in her relief at passing the course and her disinclination to engage with any further study.

Louisa is very popular with the parent group; she is from the local community and is very active in it. Her husband works at the institution that the workplace nursery supports and both her children attended the nursery. Louise was very friendly with the previous room leader who has left to take up a deputy post at another branch of the nursery.

Louisa and Fran have always worked well together, when Fran started in the toddler room Louisa was very patient and talked Fran through all of the procedures. She also confided in Fran that she found the manager of the nursery difficult to work with and 'up herself'. When the news of Fran's appointment was announced on a Thursday Louisa was off sick the next day with a stomach bug. She came back to work on Monday and congratulated Fran but was very quiet and withdrawn for the rest of the week.

The manager of the nursery, Bethany, had a long meeting with Fran when she told her of the appointment. She discussed with Fran the difficulties of Fran working with Louisa but said that she 'was sure she could pull it off'. She said that she felt that the toddler room could do with some rethinking and that there was likely to be an OFSTED inspection soon and she felt that the room needed to have some changes made so that the nursery could retain the outstanding judgment that it had gained. It was the only nursery in the chain with such a high outcome and Bethany was very keen to retain it.

Bethany told Fran that the reason that she had been appointed apart from meeting the person specific criteria and delivering a convincing interview, was that she seemed so keen to gain academic qualifications and had lots of new ideas. Bethany said that Fran had a free hand to try anything new out and that Bethany would be interested to come into the room in a couple of weeks and carry out some observations. In this meeting Bethany spoke to Fran in a very different way than she had as a practitioner.

She seemed to consider Fran more as an equal, and her, normally very business like, manner seemed more relaxed. She made some personal comments and complimented Fran on her hair colour and confided in her that she sometimes felt intimidated by Louisa as her husband had a very senior role in HR. She also said that she felt that the other two members of staff – Peter and Jola could 'do with a rocket up them' in terms of their practice.

Fran had an idea regarding the organisation of resources – she has read a lot about Maria Montessori, and wishes to help the children become more independent when selecting items. She asked the staff team to stay slightly later one day when the nursery closed to discuss her plans. It would involve some more work from the team as her scheme and reorganisation was set up and none of the staff were initially enthusiastic. Louisa sat through the meeting with her coat on and as she left Fran heard her say to Jola 'Well that won't work will it'. Fran was sure that Louisa wanted her to hear.

Reflection

Think about this case study in terms of the pressures on Fran. She has pressure both downwards and upward. Bethany is passing pressure onto Fran that she is getting from the senior management team in terms of the settings status so Fran has a burden to do well as a new appointee. She also has pressure from the other three staff, especially Louisa. Fran feels that Louisa wants Fran to fail and the other members of the team, although friendly to Fran, are not motivated enough to work against Louisa's more dominant ethos.

Fran feels that she has an upward struggle on her hands to show her true worth as a manager and leader in the room and also prove to Bethany that she deserves to be the room leader in time for Bethany's observations. Fran worries that Louisa will present the changes to the parents in a negative light.

What could Fran do?

Aggressive reaction – Fran could confront Louisa in front of the other team members and ask her what she meant by that comment. She could at the same time make reference to the way that Fran has been behaving and also share that Bethany finds it hard to work with Fran as well. All of this could be at high volume!

PROS

This might have a short-term effect of cowing Louisa into some kind of submission and acquiescence. Louisa might even feel a kind of grudging respect that Fran showed such a level of anger. The other team members might feel so scared that they also go along with Fran's plans.

CONS

This isn't a long-term sustainable reaction. Louisa has already shown that she acts in a passive-aggressive fashion and this will increase and undermine Fran and the team's cohesion. Louisa, Peter and Jola would have a case for going to Bethany and complaining about bullying if Fran continues to behave in an aggressive way. Fran's plans would not be carried out in a meaningful manner and ultimately the children's experience would suffer. It is worth restating here that all of the staff issues ultimately impact on the children's experiences in a negative or positive manner.

Bandura developed a social learning theory that proposed that behaviour can be learnt by observation and that this is applicable to children and adults. 'Emotional responses can be developed observationally by witnessing the affective reaction of others undergoing pleasurable or painful experiences' (Bandura, 1971, p. 2). In this way the adults around them are role models for children in terms of behaviour and a template for how people should interact with each other. This makes it even more important for Fran to ensure that the response that she exhibits is not aggressive if she doesn't want that behaviour reenacted in the children.

It could be argued that if this row happens when the children aren't there then they won't see it and won't be able to model it. Note though that the quote above refers to emotional responses and those would be far reaching away from the actual site of the conflict. Children would still pick up on these.

Passive

Fran could model the type of behaviour that Louisa showed. She could make comments when Louisa was in earshot to other members of the team. Comments like 'Oh some of us won't want to do this but I know that you are capable of moving a few bits of furniture even if others aren't'.

PROS

By doing this Fran is able to avoid confronting Louisa. She will be able to convey some of her feelings about the situation to Louisa without having to be direct. That might make Fran feel less anxious. By flattering the other staff members at the expense of Louisa, Fran might be able to alienate them from Louisa and get them to show loyalty to her.

CONS

Again, this type of behaviour isn't sustainable in the long run and doesn't go towards building a healthy sustainable team. Making aside comments and being sarcastic is the type of behaviour that some of us remember our least favourite teacher using and remember and feel uninspired by. We would never treat children in this way and need to remember this yardstick when we are interacting with colleagues. As well as the social learning theory we also need to remember that children have to witness 'respectful engagement' – an idea that is central to the writing of Cathy Nutbrown. (Nutbrown, 2011, p. 10). Behaving in a passive-aggressive way is not a positive model for children to emulate.

Trying to avoid confrontation with Louisa is also not sustainable in the long term, as, by behaving in this manner, we are not solving the problem. Alienating Louisa from the other team members and getting a form of reluctant loyalty from them is also not productive, as it is not based on a true sense of working as a team. Behaving in this manner will not work towards putting Fran's ideas into practice in a meaningful way or show Bethany a team who have a united sense of what effective practice looks like.

Assertive response – what this might look like

The following is our idea of what an assertive way of dealing with the issues raised in the case study might look like. There are, of course, other ways that this might be approached. We would suggest that however the detail of the response is enacted it is always based on the respectful engagement that we have highlighted. Honesty, directness and a sense of searching for common ground should underpin any interaction with team members. In this way we are more likely to find a 'win – win' outcome to a problem of communication. With a room leader, as we have already noted, the problem communication can be downward with other practitioners and upward with management.

Fran needs to make a time to see Louisa when they are both available and able to talk. That might not be at the end of the day. Bethany might have to support Fran with this by providing some cover staff to release them. In order to access this support Fran will need to talk to Bethany. She might not want at this stage to be specific about the problem with Louisa but just needs to say that she wants to have one-to-ones with all of the staff team to go through their areas of interest and possible CPD away from the bustle of the room. In fact talking to Louisa about the incident would be best framed by a general review of staff areas of strength and ways to move forward.

Presenting the interview in these terms and as something that is happening to all of the staff would then not single Louisa out from the others. This isn't a dishonest way of tackling this issue but a way of seeing it as a wider opportunity to start the team off on a positive way and with Fran being fully informed. The meeting that Fran held with the team members at the end of the day was for the sole purpose of giving them information. Fran had a plan in her head and wanted to share it with them and elicit their help. The step she has bypassed here is one of getting the team together and asking them for their ideas.

In our previous book on leadership we talk about different styles of leadership. Here, in her eagerness to put a new idea into practice, Fran has not shown a democratic style of leadership (Price and Ota, 2014) and by doing this she has not involved the team in decision making but still wanted them to support her.

At Louisa's review Fran would need to talk to her about the overheard comment. In our experience it is best to get to the point in an interview like this. When talking to a range of practitioners about difficult conversations the feedback is 'I just wanted to hear about it quickly'. It is a popular misconception that starting an interview of this sort with 'So how do you think things are going?' is a way of empowering the interviewee. In fact a remark like that causes alarm and anxiety as the practitioner searches their memory to pinpoint the cause for the critical comment that they feel is coming.

So we would recommend thanking someone for his or her time and for coming to the meeting and perhaps, as this is a general review, outlining the main agenda. We would then want to see Fran getting to the point and use the 1-2-3 point assertion technique that we outline in this book. This could be, in this case –

(1) I overheard you saying to Peter that you didn't think that my idea of rearranging the resources would work.

(2) I feel disappointed that you weren't able to tell me more detail about this so that we could iron out any problems.

(3) I hope that in the future we can speak frankly to each other about practice – I want to build a team that can compliment each other and also hold each other accountable.

After listening to Louisa's response and replying to it Fran can then go on to hear Louisa's ideas for improving the access to resources in the toddler room and ways that she wants to improve her practice. After these individual interviews Fran could arrange a team meeting, again at a time that best suits everyone. She could summarise everyone's ideas for the change and put forward a proposal to move forward on. Fran will have to accept that the end result might not be exactly as she envisaged it. The pay off here is that if it contains elements of everyone's thinking then the rest of the team are more likely to support it and carry it out.

It might be that she is not able to incorporate everyone's ideas to this change – that she feels that her way really is the best way for the children and that it shouldn't be altered in any way. If this is the case then she will have to put this forward with sound reasons – perhaps from theorists, or by linking it to the settings vision statement – why it should go ahead in its present form. She might mention the ideas that others had and propose ways of using these ideas in another form and in another project. Our advice is always to take the idea away from individual ownership and root it in best practice for children. In this way it doesn't become 'Fran's idea' that the rest of the team can oppose because they want to make a point about being told what to do, or because they resent Fran's appointment as their manager. The idea becomes best practice for children's positive outcomes – in this way opposing the idea is opposing the idea of having the best possible outcome for children.

If Fran can make this connection strong enough for the rest of the team, if she can really justify her plan in terms of it being rooted to the settings vision statement then it would be hard for anyone to find a case against it.

Conclusion

We hope that by using this case study we have achieved the aim of showing what a twofold job being a room leader is and why assertion skills are so important. Much of this discussion could also apply to practitioners working with each other and managers working with staff teams.

The argument for taking ideas away from the personal and linking them to the concept of sound outcomes for children could also be used with parents.

Working alongside staff while also being a manager is a delicate negotiation and one that supervisors in smaller settings also experience so this case study could equally apply to settings where the supervisor is not counted as extra numery. A situation where a practitioner has been promoted over resentful colleagues is equally one that could apply to a deputy or manager of a setting and requires careful handling.

In our experience honesty and a professional manner is the best way forward in most of these situations and strategies for dealing with difficult conversations and meetings can be learnt. As always we would advise role-playing and practicing before entering into any of these scenarios and keeping the well being of children at the forefront of any discussion.

References

Bandura, A. (1971) 'Social learning theory' available at http://www.esludwig.com/uploads/2/6/1/0/26105457/bandura_sociallearningtheory.pdf (accessed 13 April 2015).

Nutbrown, C. (2011) *Key concepts in early childhood education and care*, London: Sage.

Price, D. and Ota, C. (2014) *Leading and supporting early years teams*, Oxford: Routledge.

Chapter 6

Assertiveness for the early years manager

When speaking to supervisors and managers about their work we have found that the issues that keep them awake at night come not from the interaction that they have with children but the problems that they are having in their communication with other adults.

For a supervisor/manager (and we use the terms interchangeably here to mean the person in charge), the responsibility for making hard decisions and for having difficult conversations rests on their shoulders. If the staff in the setting are having difficulty communicating with each other, with parents and/or with other professionals, then the consequences of those difficulties can end up as the managers responsibility.

What was perhaps a simple case of misunderstanding or miscommunication can, through inept handling, become a serious problem by the time it reaches the managers jurisdiction. In this way the ability of the manager to be able to be clear and assertive in their communications with other adults is crucial in early years work.

We read about times where protecting the welfare of children has not had a positive outcome and there has been a tragic ending to a young life. Examples of this in recent years has been Victoria Climbie. In the report that followed the investigation into her murder one of the recommendations was:

> Recommendation 10: As part of their work, the government inspectorates should inspect both the quality of the services delivered, and also the effectiveness of the inter-agency arrangements for the provision of services to children and families.
>
> (Laming, 2003, p. 372)

Underpinning inter-agency arrangements is inter agency communication and the ability of, for the purposes of this book, the early years setting to be able to communicate effectively with social care and medical services.

Another example, more directly related to childcare settings, has been the case of the childcare practitioner at Little Teds nursery in Portsmouth who was taking pictures of children on her mobile phone and circulating them to a pedophile ring. Again, one of the recommendations was an 'urgent need to develop effective staff supervision within early years settings (6.5)' (Plymouth Safeguarding Children Board, 2010, p. 34). While the two cases seem unrelated and the recommendations very different, we believe that there is an underpinning similarity between them in that there is an issue of poor communication that is common. Effective multi-agency working is highlighted in all of the reports that have been written after a national child protection scandal has been revealed.

We believe that good assertion skills are part of a wider effective communication practice and would help agencies talk to each other and, especially, early years settings engage in a culture of clear communication that is led by the manager. The manager should be able to establish a community where all staff, including themselves, are accountable for their practice. In order to sustain this the manager needs to lead by modeling a high order of communication skills. We think that assertion skills are an integral part of this practice.

Case study

Bev is the manager of a large day care nursery. The room leader of the baby room, Lucy, has recently been to see her with concerns about Ruth, one of the practitioners in the room. Ruth has been chatting to one of the mothers of the babies when the parent has come to pick her child up. The child is called Daisy and she is six months old. The parent has returned to work reluctantly and the child has been at the nursery full time for three days a week for a month. The mother is young and this is her first child. She has been in tears regularly when she leaves her child and often phones the nursery during the day to check and see how Daisy is.

Ruth is an older woman who has a large family of her own. Lucy was initially pleased to see Ruth and the parent talking so freely with one another and felt that Ruth was a valuable resource for the mother. Yesterday though, she heard Ruth telling the mother to let Daisy cry if she woke at night and she also expressed an opinion that babies 'knew what they were doing' and were 'manipulative'.

Lucy is a recently qualified level 3 practitioner who does not have children and she feels unconfident about tackling Ruth about this incident.

What would you do?

It is difficult to give a 'right' answer here. Case studies are not multiple-choice questions and there are many resolutions to this problem, all have some benefits to the situation. The response does depend on the participants involved, the style of leadership that Bev feels comfortable with and the reactions from individuals to the intervention. We also have to think of short term and long-term solutions to this problem. In the short term there has to be a response to the advice that Ruth is giving this parent, as it is ill advised and not in line with good child development practice.

In the long term there are issues about Ruth's understanding of child development and also her idea of being a professional practitioner who can use her own experiences of being a mother while still maintaining a professional demeanor with parents.

There are also issues around Bev's confidence as a manager of the baby room and how she can assert herself and make sure that she is able to direct all of the staff effectively in their practice.

Finally there is some self-reflection here. As a manager was it a good decision to put Ruth in the baby room knowing her background and personality and being aware of the capacities of the newly qualified Lucy.

Extra background

There is also always extra information that is not detailed in the initial summing up of a situation and questions we should be asking if we are going to think of a reflective answer to the issues. One of the underpinning skills in assertion techniques is to resist being rushed into responding to a situation but if at all possible to take control by choosing a time and place that feel like they will enable a positive outcome. Some of these questions would be:

- What kind of relationship do Lucy and Ruth have? Did Ruth apply for the room leaders job and was Lucy selected instead of her?
- What kind of relationship do Bev and Ruth have? Has Ruth been at the nursery longer than any other member of staff and seen people being promoted over her?
- How long has Ruth been working in the baby room and does her training equip her to work there.

Some answers to these questions:

- Lucy and Ruth do get on well as long as Lucy agrees with Ruth. Ruth sees Lucy as a kind of daughter figure who needs guidance even though she is in charge of the baby room and technically manages Ruth.
- Bev and Ruth have a difficult relationship as they used to be equal colleagues; indeed Ruth was Bev's mentor when she initially started working at the nursery. Ruth has seen Bev rise to room leader, deputy manager and now manager over the years. Ruth repeatedly says that she 'doesn't want any responsibility' and states loudly in the staff room that with her large family she wants to 'leave the job at the door when I leave thanks very much'. Bev had to put a lot of pressure on Ruth to complete her level 3 qualification. Ruth completed it in house and Bev sometimes worries that she didn't take in a lot of the material and doesn't use her studies in her practice.
- Ruth has just started in the baby room. She asked to be placed there because she said that she was fed up with the paperwork of the rising 5's and thought that the babies would involve less recording. Bev heard Ruth in the staff room telling another member of staff that 'My own babies are all at school now and I miss the cuddles'.

Now there is more information to reflect on. We would always advise a period of information gathering before taking action if at all possible.

Next steps

Both members of staff need supporting here. Bev needs supporting in order to address the issues that she is concerned about with Ruth and assert herself as a room leader. It would be tempting as the manager of the nursery to seek a meeting with Ruth and talk to her about the conversation that Bev overheard. In fact that could undermine Bev as the room leader and we would suggest that the best way to resolve the situation would be to discuss a range of assertive strategies that Bev could adopt in order to manage Ruth and extend her practice. We would suggest that when talking to Bev the following points need thinking about.

- The separation from the particular incident to critiques of Ruth practice. This means that each needs to be dealt with separately. For example, starting a conversation with Ruth by saying 'I heard your conversation with Daisy's mother and it's not acceptable to give her that kind of advice. Also I don't think that you really understand child development in regard to working with babies'. If Bev does this she is overwhelming Ruth with her criticisms and Ruth is far more likely to be defensive in return. Bev is also making it harder to discuss either the incident or the general concerns specifically.

- Making it clear that the advice that Ruth gave is not acceptable early on in the exchange. There can be a tendency to try and disguise unwelcome news with praise. We have discussed this elsewhere in this book and this incident is a clear example of where this has to be avoided. As practitioners we need to praise each other's practice in the same way that we praise children's achievements. If we use this praise in order to make difficult observations more palatable then we demean the praise and the received is likely to be suspicious of it as in 'Yes she said that she liked my displays but then went onto comment that I should involve children more in them. Because of that I don't think that she really meant it when she gave me praise'. The receiver can also just stop at the praise and not hear the comment afterward as in 'yes she thought my displays were great, oh and something about the children but it wasn't that important'.
- Working with Ruth to find out what she likes about the work in the baby room and how she feels that she can improve her practice.
- Being clear about the expectations of Ruth's practice as a room leader.

Time, space and practical arrangements for discussions

It is clear that, in order to deal with this situation effectively there will have to be a one-to-one exchange. This will have to be with Bev and may also have to be with Ruth if Bev feels unable to deal with the situation even with support. It is important to set up the practical arrangements for this meeting or meetings and think about the physical layout as well as the content.

One of the underpinning precepts of assertion is that it is important to choose a time and a place if possible that suit the person initiating the interchange and provides a space that enable both parties to reach a comfortable solution to the issue.

If a manager confronts a practitioner in a public place, in front of colleagues or parents then both parties may feel defensive. In this case the issues that are being discussed will be affected and manipulated by other hidden agendas. This could be the managers need to assert authority in front of parents – to show parents that they are in control of the staff team and that the parents can have confidence in the management of the setting. If this is in front of other members of staff then the manager may be trying to show staff that they are a strong leader who won't be afraid to take action and won't back down.

It could be that this scenario is being played out to show a particular member of staff that they need to watch their behaviour in the future. It could be that the manager has had an unsatisfactory exchange with a member of staff and wants to make amends for this by showing clearly in this interchange that they can be assertive and powerful.

Similarly the staff member, if spoken to in a public place may feel the need to react far more defensively than they would in a more private interview. They may not want to show their colleagues that they have any doubts about their own behaviour or actions and that they are able to have a confrontation with the manager and gain the upper hand.

We can see by this that just choosing a private space can allow both participants to just deal with the issues that are relevant and can cut away many of the other ingredients that could cloud any progression to a truthful and honest interchange where both parties can speak freely without fear of recrimination or judgments from others.

Time is also important. At the end of a long busy day both parties will not be performing at the peak of their abilities and the practitioner may agree to actions just to be able to call a halt to the discussion and be able to go home. Even the beginning of the day can be a problem if the manager has a long 'to do' list that is at the front of their thinking and moving them towards swift completion of the interview rather than a full exploration of attitudes and feelings.

These are practical considerations but it is important to have a space where both parties can sit comfortably and, if possible, at an equal height so that they look each other in the eye when talking.

Activity

With a colleague try and have a discussion (not a serious one) between you where you are positioned differently. Try a

- children's chair when one person is in an adult chair
- sitting on the edge of a desk while one person is in an adult chair
- standing next to someone who is sitting in an adult's chair
- and all of the possibilities above mixed up – try a beanbag!

Reflection

Hopefully you can see the difference in the power dynamics that can happen just by using different seating. When talking to children we try and get down to their level so that they don't feel intimidated. Similarly with colleagues we need to make sure that we can sit and look each other in the eye from an equal height so that our body language isn't giving any messages of inferiority or superiority that might affect our language or how it is being received.

Summary of practical considerations

In taking care of time, space and positioning we can make sure that we are doing the absolute best that we can in order to provide a forum where difficult and sensitive subjects can be addressed and discussed in an assertive and open way. The most effective way that we can enable this is to take care of easily adjusted practical considerations that only need a little thought and arranging. Of course setting up an emotionally healthy environment that equally provides a nurturing and safe space for assertive behaviour to happen in can take more time and effort.

From this case study we hope that you can see the layers of meaning and action that are involved in what, at first glance, might seem a straightforward situation. Being an effective leader does involve a high level of assertion skills in order to manage a myriad of different situations with staff, parents and external agencies. However it is not always the best strategy to jump in and deal with a situation personally. Part of being an effective leader and manager is the ability to empower others to be assertive rather than act on their behalf. In the case study above it might be that Lucy, even with support, is not able to deal with the situation with Ruth and so, as a manager you may have to step in and act. However the most effective and long-term situation would be to enable Lucy to be able to set up an assertive relationship with Ruth where she can work with her as a team member and also make it clear what her expectations are as a room leader.

This is a short term/long term strategy as it is tempting to get a short-term solution by dealing with the situation. To achieve a long-term solution though, Lucy needs to be skilled in managing the staff in the baby room in an assertive way. By achieving this goal we, as a manager, are not only providing a solution to the problem of managing Ruth, but also enabling Lucy to manage the other staff more effectively, now and in the future.

Of course, the ideal situation here would be to ensure that all staff are able to act assertively so that as a manager we can hold them accountable and have confidence in their ability to work effectively with each other and build and maintain open and honest relationships with us and with each other.

Finally, we are aware that all of this advance preparation is not always possible and, especially for managers, sometimes swift responses are necessary when dealing with members of staff and difficult situations. We are aware that the paramount concern is the safety and welfare of the child and that this has to be the underpinning of any response and be the first directive.

We hope though, that you can see that ensuring that staff are able to act assertively is part of being an assertive leader, and provides the backbone of a well functioning and acting staff team who are effectively managed. If this is in place then, even with situations that are a crisis, responses will be clearer and more thoughtful and there will be damage limitation.

References

Laming, H. (2003) 'The Victoria Climbie inquiry' available at https://www.gov.uk/government/uploads/system/uploads/attachment_data/file/273183/5730.pdf (accessed 13 April 2015).

Plymouth Safeguarding Children Board, (2010) 'Serious case review overview report executive summary in respect of nursery Z' available at http://www.plymouth.gov.uk/serious_case_review_nursery_z.pdf (accessed 13 April 2015).

Part 3

Developing it

Chapter 7

Equipping children with the skills

Having explored the landscape of assertiveness and its usefulness for early years practitioners and teams, this chapter will consider how assertiveness can also benefit children in a setting; offering a valuable opportunity to enrich their relationships with peers and adults and extend their communication, independence and problem-solving skills.

Why?

In 'Development Matters', the non-statutory guidance that supports the statutory EYFS, there is a focus on personal, social and emotional development: making relationships (Moylett and Stewart, 2012). Clearly assertion skills support and enhance the relationships that children have with each other. Furthermore in the EYFS it states as one of the four aims that 'children learn to be strong and independent through positive relationships' (Department for Education, 2014, p. 6). Communication and relationships are at the heart of policy and guidance within the early years curriculum and assertion skills are crucial in establishing, developing and enhancing these skills between children.

As well as affirmed through early years best practice and policy, assertiveness as a problem-solving and communication tool is consistent with and encouraged through the vision, mission statements and aims of many early years settings. For any setting that promotes and professes values around inclusion, respect and belonging, assertiveness offers a practical strategy for living out those values and making it a reality.

In enabling individuals to take responsibility for themselves, how they feel and what they want or need, assertiveness supports inclusive settings who seek to ensure respect and an environment where everyone has the right to belong, contribute and feel valued, whatever their age. Assertiveness, as we have seen, is a strong foundation for good communication: it develops empathy, resilience and establishes avenues for developing constructive conflict. Where early years practitioners and settings take first steps in offering children the possibility to see assertiveness modelled, learn and practice it, they are providing a valuable opportunity for children to be supported in the setting in their relationships with adults around them and their peers.

In building the practical strategies, key scripts, attitudes and awareness of assertiveness, even very young children can be better supported in being able to engage with others. This benefit, of course, extends beyond their time in early years.

Laying the foundations and early skills for assertiveness develops an open mind set for children, boosting their self-esteem, independence and confidence as they transition into school and beyond to adulthood and later life.

For the early years practitioners still developing their own confidence and understanding of assertiveness it may be daunting to also think about how it could work and be implemented with very young children. Others may consider children in early years simply too young to engage with assertiveness. We address this now by considering how assertiveness can fit with and support early years settings.

A place for assertiveness in early years

Conflict exists

Our starting point is that conflict exists across all ages, even with very young children. You only have to observe two children at loggerheads wanting the same toy to see it in action. So if conflict, and disagreeing with each other, exist across all ages, the bigger question is how is it is addressed and resolved? For example, if two children are head-to-head wanting the same toy truck to play with, what happens next? There are a number of different scenarios that might play out:

(1) With no one else around and left to themselves, the children might shout, hit and cry until one backs down and the other (usually the loudest, strongest and more powerful one) gets their way.
(2) The children may argue for a bit, perhaps fight or start crying until an adult notices and intervenes.

(3) The children might realise they can't resolve it on their own and seek out an adult to resolve the situation for them.

(4) An adult observing the children coming together, and anticipating the potential flashpoint for conflict, may pre-empt an escalation of the conflict by intervening.

In (1) above the children independently resolve the situation, even if it is not in the most positive way. In scenarios (2), (3) and (4) an adult is needed to help the children sort out the situation. There are different ways an early years practitioner could take this forward:

(a) Use distraction and offer an alternative toy.

(b) Separate the children to different areas to play with something else.

(c) Stay in the situation with the toy they both want and offer suggestions for resolving the situation. For example, suggesting they take turns or use a sand timer.

(d) Stay in the situation with the toy they both want and use labeling, modeling, questioning and facilitation to help the children recognise and address the conflict and try and find a way to resolve the situation.

Whilst (c) might be preferable to (a) or (b), there are further significant benefits of option (d) above where instead of something being done **to** the children (adult sorts it out), the conflict is addressed and resolved **with** them. Broadly speaking in (d), the situation becomes a learning opportunity for the children to:

• understand how people interact and might disagree with each other

• hear and learn key vocabulary for describing conflict and how they feel

• see how situations of conflict can be resolved though talking, listening, negotiation and compromise

• become active participants in addressing the situation of conflict and finding a resolution

• practice and learn strategies and scripts they can use again and transfer to other contexts and situations.

Even with very young children it is possible for the practitioner to model and label the situation as a resolution is found (Ota and Vollick, 2011). We acknowledge that whilst there may always be a place for adults to intervene and use strategies of separating or distracting children to resolve conflict, we would urge practitioners to reflect and consider the deeper motives and reasons why this is used.

Let us consider an arts and craft scenario. Rarely would it seem acceptable for an early years practitioner to intervene on a child painting, pick up the paintbrush and complete the picture for them. It may be quicker and easier to finish the picture yourself but that misses the point of the child having the experience and learning from it. In the same way situations of conflict and disagreeing with others are important opportunities for children experience the world, engage with others and learn. It may be quicker and easier to sort out an argument between children to separate and distract them, however, promoting independence, showing and teaching the children how to do it for themselves is clearly preferred in terms of the longer term learning and benefits.

How can assertiveness help?

Employing the framework and three steps of assertiveness we have explored in previous chapters let us return to the two children wanting to play with the same toy truck. How can an early years practitioner utilise assertiveness to structure their intervention with the children? Addressing each child in the pair and giving both of them the chance to speak, the three steps of the intervention could proceed as follows:

(1) Establish what is happening, keeping to the facts - what is going on? It looks like. . . . It sounds as if you both want to play with this truck.
(2) Identify how each child is feeling - so how do you feel about that? Can you tell (name) how you feel about that? It looks like you're feeling. . . .
(3) Determine what each child needs or wants - so (name) can you tell (other child) what you want? What would you like?

We see here that this brings us to a point where although the situation might still not be resolved, the practitioner has prevented any further escalation and helped the children both take responsibility for the problem. From here the practitioner can ask each child for suggestions about what they could do next (How can we sort this out? What can we do?) and hopefully this will provide a route forward for resolving the difficulty.

There are a number of observations that can be made about the role of the early years practitioner in this scenario and how they engage with the children, they:

- introduce the vocabulary and use it appropriately for the context
- reinforce listening skills and turn taking to maintain dialogue
- use open-ended questions to engage the children and encourage them to reflect and think
- enable the children to identify how they feel and tell the other person
- encourage the children to take responsibility how they feel
- model, prompts and create an environment for finding a win-win situation
- promote independence and resect for others
- facilitates and supports both of the children in finding a solution together.

Most importantly the adult in this scenario is able to maintain the connection and communication between the two children. Often when adults intervene in a situation between children the connection and communication between the children is severed as they both turn their attention and focus to the adult. Where the adult is able to facilitate and maintain the connection between the children the dialogue is sustained between the children and in a supported and scaffolded way, they can experience and learn from peer-to-peer communication and conflict resolution.

If relationships with peers and adults are improved when children are encouraged to explore and practice the steps of assertiveness communication and behaviour, this inevitably also has the potential to more broadly impact on their collaborative and cooperative learning together. In extending thinking skills and building what Carol Dweck describes as 'executive functioning' children can be more flexible, adaptable and creative.

The fundamental role of practitioners

Where we can make a strong case for developing assertiveness with young children it clearly is dependent on the understanding and skills of the early years. We have outlined a broad range of general skills above and in addition to this it is essential that practitioners have themselves a clear understanding of how to appropriately bring assertiveness into their professional practice with children. This is where a whole setting approach to learning about, practicing and developing assertiveness is helpful. Where assertiveness is valued as part of an ethos of respect and effective communication it can support both practitioners and children in developing their confidence, understanding and skills (Ota and Vollick, 2011).

For children to learn and practice assertiveness practitioners need to fundamentally value and give time to assertiveness as a means of effective communication. In addition they need to:

(1) know building blocks of skills and understanding that make up assertive communication
(2) create and look for opportunities for children to explicitly practice and learn strategies, vocabulary and skills
(3) embed and integrate opportunities for using assertive communication throughout daily routine and all learning.

Evidence from across the UK and internationally continues to challenge our assumptions as adults about what children are capable of in terms of empathy, skills, relationships and independence. Working in Canada for the last decade with children as young as 6 months we, and the experienced practitioners we have worked with, have continued to be challenged by how very young children have surprised us and surpassed our expectations. This is worth reminding ourselves, frequently. Often our own expectations limit what our children are capable of; we need to revisit our assumptions regularly to ensure that it is us who are preventing our children from being and doing so much more (Ota and Vollick, 2011).

Practical suggestions for first steps and putting assertiveness in place for children

Although assertiveness can be broken down into three apparently simple steps of communication it nevertheless requires a range of complex skills, vocabulary and understanding. As discussed in Chapter 2, we can locate the ability to use assertiveness communication with the broader landscape of relational intelligence, that is, the ability to connect, respect and maintain connection and relationships with others.

Whilst the benefits of acquiring the skills, attitudes and ability to utilize assertiveness might be easy to recognize, it can be more difficult to determine the 'how' of making it happen. In the last chapters we will be unpicking how different building blocks of relational intelligence can provide a practical way forward for developing assertiveness with both children and practitioners.

In our earlier example of two children in conflict over the same toy, we explored how assertiveness might look and sound and be supported with very young children. In order to engage in this requires some even more basic skills such as appropriate eye contact, taking turns, listening and disagreeing politely. Indeed the list is extensive, and goes on even longer, when we break down the constituent elements that need to come together for the process to succeed.

For the purposes of this exploration we offer five key building blocks as first steps in building the environment and developing the skills for children to engage with and develop assertiveness:

(1) Appropriate eye contact
(2) Knowing and using names
(3) Listening as stopping and be ready to listen
(4) Listening as remembering
(5) Making decisions together.

We have broken down each building block under a series of headings:

- What it is – a brief overview of what that skill is and how it can help.
- Key vocabulary – recognising the importance of words to describe, label and talk about the skill.
- Useful phrases – ideas for practising and teaching key phrases related to a skill
- How to practice it – games provide an opportunity for children to see the skill in action, label it and practice it for themselves. We offer suggestions for games that explicitly and intentionally highlight and focus on that specific skill.

Trust as the very first step

When groups and children come together, trust is the very first starting point for them to be able to engage and connect. To facilitate, encourage and support this we suggest here two building blocks of skills:

1. Eye contact

What it is: eye contact helps people connect, focus and communicate with each other. More accurately this is appropriate eye contact: understanding and appreciating the importance of looking at someone when they are talking to you or you are talking to them. It is knowing the difference between 'scary staring' and looking out the window when you are talking – appropriate eye contact is about facing and looking at the person you're communicating with.

Key vocabulary: look, eyes, magnet eyes, watch, see, not staring.

How to practice it: regular modelling and labelling by practitioners is the most effective way for children to observe and see eye contact around them. Suggestions for games:

- try looking in a mirror and making eye contact with yourself;
- pass the teddy and look at the teddy;
- sit in pairs, knees touching, look at each other, make eye contact and smile/give a high five/say good morning
- pass the smile/good morning/thumbs up/hand shake around the circle and be sure to make eye with the person as you do so.

Where eye contact is difficult children can be encouraged to look at the top of someone's head or their eyebrows.

2. Knowing and using names

What it is: it is easy to assume that children who have been together for months, if not years, will all know each other's names. Explicitly focusing on ensuring everyone knows everyone else's name, can pronounce it correctly and use it regularly is an easy, practical way of building greater inclusion and respect.

Key vocabulary: name, who, say your name

Useful phrases: What is your name? My name is. . . . My friends name is . . . This is. . . .

How to practice it: again regular modelling and labelling by practitioners is the most effective way for children to observe and see eye contact around them. Suggestions for games:

- good morning circle, saying hello and good morning (name) to the person either side of them
- jack in the box – go round a circle say your own name and then repeat introducing person either side of you – 'my name is _ and this is _ and this is _'
- this is for you – role play giving someone else an imaginary present, saying 'this is for you (name)'

- space on my right – sit in a circle with one space on your right. Begin game by saying 'I have a space on my right and I would like (name) to come and sit here'. The person with the vacate spot on their right continues the game by repeating the phrase and inviting someone to come and sit on the right.

Communication

We offer here three further building blocks that can help in taking first steps to building assertiveness with children. Where attention to trust can help children connect, engage and focus with each other, these three building blocks help children communicate more effectively.

3. Active listening as stopping and being ready to listen

What it is: listening is difficult. More than just being quiet or waiting for you turn to jump in and talk, active, richer listening involves more demanding skills and the first important step is being able to stop and be ready to listen. Practicing stopping and being quiet helps children focus and be ready to listen; it helps them understand that listening is an active rather than passive process.

Key vocabulary: stop, ready, listen, hear, listening ears; listening eyes

Useful phrases: I am listening; I'm ready; show me you are ready

How to practice it: alongside the modelling and labelling of the practitioners games to practice this include:

- musical statues
- Chinese whispers around a circle
- quietly sitting and watching a shaken snow globe settle until its still
- mirroring games in pairs where one person mirrors their partner's actions (hand movements/facial expressions).

4. Active listening as remembering

What it is: building on stopping and being ready to listen, listening is remembering reinforces the understanding an awareness that listening is an active rather than passive process. Assertive communication between children as a tool for conflict resolution requires then to the two listen to each other as well as express and talk about how they feel and what they want. In order to accomplish this they need to be to remember what the other person has said!

Key vocabulary: remember, repeat, echo

Phrases you might use: he/she/you said that . . . how did . . . when . . . can you tell me one thing your partner told you?

How to practice it:

- rhythm games
- name train
- action rhymes and songs
- going to the market/packing a suitcase memory games.

5. Making decisions together

What it is: we include this more complex skill as a final building block as an example how initial stepping stones can progress to more complex skills. 'Making decisions together' raises awareness of decisions can be made together in a respectful and constructive way. It is a more complex and demanding skill that progresses on from the previous building blocks we have discussed.

Key vocabulary: decision, honest, agree, disagree, choose, compromise, consequence

Phrases you might use: I think . . . because . . . ; Have you thought about . . . ? Can I just say. . . .

How to practice it:

- compromise games
- in pairs choose between two options (e.g. dog or cat? Apple or orange?)
- sharing resources for construction or craft activities
- joint art/craft project – what are you going to make/draw and how are you going to decide?

Further practical suggestions for assertiveness with children

Assertiveness as we have explored in this book brings together these five building blocks with many others. It is recommended that time be spent establishing the basic blocks of trust and communication before the much higher complex skills of assertiveness are tackled. Where practitioners are looking to practice bringing together the different strands and skills of assertiveness with children, we offer the following prompts to consider when introducing and practising the skills.

(1) What is the key vocabulary the children will need to talk about and label assertiveness?
(2) What phrases/scripts would be useful for the children to know and practice?
(3) What simple games will help children identify, experience, talk about and practice elements of assertiveness?
(4) Where could you embed this across the daily routine and learning environment?

References

Center for the Developing Child, Harvard University (2015) 'InBrief: Executive Function: Skills for Life and Learning' (Video), available at http://develop ingchild.harvard.edu/resources/multimedia/videos/inbrief_series/inbrief_execu tive_function/ (accessed 3 May 2015).

Department for Education (2014) *Statutory framework for the early years foundation stage: Setting the standards for learning, development and care for children from birth to five*, London: Department for Education.

Moylett, H. and Stewart, N. (2012) *Development matters in the early years foundation stage (EYFS)*, London: Early Education.

Ota, C. and Vollick, M. P. (2011) 'Inspiring values, skills, confidence and communities – a case study of a social, relational approach to religious education and spirituality in the early years', *Journal of Religious Education* 59(2): 23–34.

Chapter 8

Developing the broader climate

In this chapter we will consider how early years practitioners, teams and settings can take their first steps together in moving towards establishing assertiveness as a tool for effective communication. We will explore this by referring to both the early years practitioner as part of a team and how those with leadership responsibilities can further enhance and support this.

Each team and every early years setting has its own unique profile and dynamics. Likewise, an individual, early years setting and team will need to identify its own personal starting point in order to ascertain the most appropriate stepping stones and first steps for establishing assertiveness. This chapter can only speak in general terms and signpost key elements that, in our experience, have enabled teams and settings to create the climate for assertiveness to evolve and usefully strengthen and improve their team and setting. Regardless of wherever a person, team or setting find themselves it is an attitude of openness, flexibility of mind and willingness to reflect and do things differently that will enable any change to happen. Recognising our suggestions may present different levels of challenge for practitioners who may feel uncomfortable or unfamiliar with the material, we offer some reflective question prompts and practical suggestions to assist in your reflections.

For early years practitioners

We start with focusing on what an individual early years practitioner can do to lay the necessary foundations for developing their confidence and skills, so that they can be more assertive in their professional practice. These first steps mirror the process described in Chapter 7 for developing assertiveness with children. The principles for building positive relationships and effective communication remain the same, despite the difference in age.

Pay attention to building trust

Trust is the bedrock of any relationship and team. When practitioners are consciously mindful of connecting with others and sustaining that trust there is a solid foundation for enabling constructive difficult conversations and assertiveness. Two further thoughts on trust. Firstly, it is easily overlooked, disregarded or taken for granted and secondly, somewhat inevitably, there will be occasions and times when trust gets dented or knocked (Price and Ota, 2014, p. 65). What is important in both instances is that time and attention is given to maintaining and building trust. This is far more impactful than merely presuming it will somehow just happen.

The early years practitioner can build trust by giving attention to the same basic behaviours and core communication skills that we discussed for children: appropriate eye contact and knowing and using names is an easy place to start. As with our assumption that children will, of course, know each other's names if they have been together in the same room for over a year, it is easy to assume we do this already. Yet being more aware of our interactions with others and intentionally using more of these two skills, we can observe two things, that: (1) we don't use it as much as we could and (2) doing it better and more regularly in our interactions with colleagues, children and parents can make a positive and significant difference in the professionalism, quality and positivity of our interactions.

Suggestions and questions prompts:

(1) Are there colleagues or parents that I find it difficult to make eye contact with?
(2) Why do I find it uncomfortable?
(3) When I speak with children do I get to their level and make eye contact each time or am I distracted and doing something else at the same time?

(4) Do I know the name of every child? The parents and carers?
(5) Do I know the name of all my colleagues?
(6) Are there other names I can learn and use?
(7) Can I use names more in my everyday communication?

Why not try:

- If eye contact is uncomfortable try looking at someone's head or eyebrows
- Using photos of children or families as prompts to learn names
- Using names more often than you are used to, for example when saying 'hello', 'good morning', 'can you . . . ' and 'thank you'
- Practice, practice, practice eye contact – in a mirror, in safer places like going shopping or with friends and family
- Practice, practice, practice knowing and using names – introduce yourself to parents and children, ask them their name.

Listen

In building on these first two steps we can continue along the same path that was presented for children in Chapter 7 by giving our attention to becoming better listeners. To truly listen to another person is active and it is difficult, particularly within the busy pace and multiple demands that can fill a working day. Often we are not listening to others but simply biding our time until we can get on with our next job or have our turn to speak. Breaking down the matrix of skills needed to be a better listener starts with being present to the other person, as we saw with children one first step for this is stopping and being ready to listen. Again this sounds easy, nevertheless, it is only when we tune in and develop more awareness of how we behave and speak that we often begin to see that this is harder than it first appears.

Only when a person is able to stop and be ready to listen can more effective listening take place, for example, being able to remember what the person just said. We suggest this as an additional communication building block that can greatly enhance interactions and relationships within a team and for a setting. In remembering what a person has said it is then possible to reflect back, build on an idea, ask relevant questions and give feedback.

These two communication skills are a further step for the early years practitioner to practice and develop as they seek to lay the foundations for greater confidence and skills in using assertiveness.

Suggestions and questions prompts:

(1) Can I stop completely and be still?
(2) When I stop moving is my head still buzzing and chatting inside? Can I stop that too?
(3) What do I notice around me when I stop? What can I see? Hear?
(4) When someone is talking to me can I remember two things they just told me?
(5) Can I summarise a couple of key points someone told me and ask a relevant question about it or build on their idea?

Why not try:

- Stopping and counting slowly to 10 noticing and being aware of your breath
- Sitting still, just for a minute
- Noticing how often you are in the present moment – or are you focusing on what has happened in the past or what might happen/planning for the future
- Recalling what some tells you and reflecting it back to yourself or them
- Practice, practice, practice – being still, stopping everything for a just moment, for a count of 10
- Practice, practice, practice – remembering and reminding yourself what someone has just told you; remembering what someone told you earlier in the day.

Figure out how you feel

We now detour somewhat from the path set out for children in Chapter 7 by suggesting three other ways early years practitioners can support themselves and develop their professional practice. These are focused on developing greater self-awareness and attention to what we are thinking and feeling as well as what we are doing and saying.

Using an 'I' message and being able to say how you feel is a core component of the three steps of assertiveness communication and so this is an important aspect of self-awareness for practitioners to develop. One way to enhance this is to extend our understanding of emotions. Like children we often use only a limited, narrow range of vocabulary to describe how we are feeling; sometimes no more than happy, sad, angry, disappointed, upset. The English language has a list of over a hundred words to describe different emotions and so familiarising ourselves with these and using them to identify and describe how we are feeling can benefit greatly in helping us and others recognise how we feel. Emotions also vary in intensity and again it can be useful to remind and ask ourselves whether the feelings we are having are at a low, medium or high intensity.

Stopping and being ready to listen, mentioned above, also works here for supporting the early years practitioner in knowing how they feel. Noticing how you feel often means a person has to pause, stop and connect with that feeling so they can identify it. There is no need to judge it (e.g. 'I shouldn't feel that way' or 'that's wrong'), it's about just noticing it's there and giving it a name.

Suggestions and questions prompts:

(1) How many emotion words do I use?
(2) How am I feeling?

Why not try:

•   Finding a list of emotions vocabulary (there are plenty of free ones on the Internet) – tick off the words you already use and find three new words that you think would be useful for you
•   Stopping for a moment and asking yourself how you feel.

Be ready to take responsibility

As well as naming how they feel, the three steps of assertiveness require a person to take responsibility for themselves, the situation they find themselves in and what they want. Before being able to communicate and speak about that with another person, an individual has to know for themselves what they want. One reason why this can prove problematic is that we don't give the time to really knowing what we think and want, all we know is that we feel angry, bothered or simply want it to be different to how it is.

A further barrier to knowing ourselves and what we want is that we believe that others should just 'know' us and what we want; in effect this is akin to expecting colleagues, children and others around us to be mind readers. This is both unfair and unrealistic, and means we avoid taking responsibility for ourselves. The same strategies we presented above, to identify how one is feeling, serve to enable the practitioner to also discern what is going on and happening (step 1 of assertiveness – the facts) and what they want or need to happen (step 3).

Extending self-awareness and acknowledging how we feel, think and what we want breaks down the different elements needed for assertive communication and can help the practitioner gain more confidence in bringing them together and professionally deliver assertive messages.

Reflect on your own communication style for conflict

Embedding into professional practice the key elements above is a practical, effective way of taking individual steps towards developing our professional practice and integrating assertiveness into a repertoire of effective communication and problem solving strategies. There are many more components of communication building blocks that come together in assertive communication and in Chapter 9 we will examine more complex skills that can be introduced and practiced as a team to support this.

A final and useful signpost for laying the groundwork for assertiveness is to notice and reflect one's own preferred communication style in a situation of conflict. In Chapters 3–6 we described the ways early years practitioners in different roles might respond and communicate in difficult situations. Through the examples provided we encouraged the reader to look and see where they might notice themselves and their own behaviours. In reviewing possible passive, aggressive and passive aggressive responses we also described how communication could be framed and structured to deliver messages assertively.

We will build on this now to consider practical ways in which the early years practitioner can extend their own awareness and understanding of how they communicate in difficult situations – and take steps to shift towards more assertive positive and professional communication.

Chapters 2–6 describe in detail the different features of passive, aggressive and passive aggressive communication. Here are some practical suggestions for identifying your own preferred style and what you could try to change how you communicate.

Passive – saying too little; aim to avoid conflict

Suggestions and questions prompts:

(1) Do you speak apologetically or softly?
(2) Do you struggle to make eye contact with others?
(3) When in a difficult situation do you find yourself giving into what others want without objecting, just for a quiet life?
(4) Do others respond to me by. . . .

Aggressive – saying too much; aim to get their own way, regardless of thoughts, feelings or opinions of others

Suggestions and questions prompts:

(1) Do you speak loudly?
(2) Do you try and dominate others?
(3) Are you prone to criticism, blame or attacking others?
(4) When in a difficult situation do I find myself. . . . ?
(5) Do others respond to me by . . . ?

Why not try:

• Stopping and waiting to listening to the other person
• Ask questions.

Passive aggressive – saying one thing (passive) and doing something else (aggressive)

Suggestions and questions prompts:

(1) Do you find it difficult to be honest and tell others what I think and feel?
(2) Do you agree to do something and then pretend to forget or not follow through?
(3) Do you frequently feel resentful, blame others, avoiding responsibility and complain about being misunderstood and unappreciated?
(4) Do you find that I might ignore someone for a period of time but not tell them why?

Why not try:

- Identifying when and where you use this behaviour, what are the triggers?
- Cutting out scarcasm from what you say (Siegmund, 2015, p. 27)
- Be responsible for your feelings by saying 'I feel . . . ' – no exceptions (Murphy and Hoff Oberlin, 2005, p. 189)
- Focus on resolution rather than attack.

For early years leaders and managers

As with any early years practitioner, whatever their role, a leader and manager in an early years setting has to begin by considering their own confidence, understanding and skills in using assertiveness. The steps described above can serve as a strong foundation for starting out.

Alongside this pathway for moving forwards themselves, the early years leader and manager also has to acknowledge their vital role in consistently and explicitly modelling the component building blocks for assertiveness for staff and the setting. Their position in the organisation puts them in a situation of considerable influence; modeling the behaviour and communication you want to see more of is one of the most effective ways of reinforcing the message for staff and setting clear expectations as well as encouraging and supporting colleagues.

The twofold task for early years leaders and managers is to not only consider their own skills and personal development, but also how they enable colleagues and their team to developing the skills and confidence needed for assertiveness to be embedded across a setting and used as productively as an organisation.

Implementing any long-term and sustainable change across a setting and staff team takes time. Besides modeling assertiveness with colleagues, leaders and managers can also reinforce expectations and encourage staff in their efforts to communicate more effectively. Taking a step by step approach to building the confidence and skills of staff, leaders and managers can support on a one to one basis through informal everyday interactions as well as using the opportunities provided by appraisals, supervision and other meetings. In the following chapter we will consider how team working together can support each other in developing assertiveness as a whole setting approach and ethos.

References

Murphy, T. and Hoff Oberlin, L. (2005) *Overcoming passive–aggression: how to stop hidden anger from spoiling your relationships, career and happiness*, Philadelphia: Da Capo Press.

Price, D. and Ota, C. (2014) *Leading and supporting early years teams*, Oxford: Routledge.

Siegmund, L. (2015) *Passive aggressive: living with passive aggressive behaviour*, Canada: Create Space.

Chapter 9

Embedding, sustaining and developing assertiveness in your practice and setting

In Chapter 8 we explored how the individual early years practitioner could take practical steps towards developing their skills and confidence in using assertiveness. We also began to look at how the early years leader and manager can support their staff by both modeling and working 1:1 with colleagues to reinforce and encourage assertiveness skills. This chapter will extend this discussion to consider the benefits and practicalities of early years teams working together to develop assertive communication as an organization and setting-wide approach.

As with Chapters 7 and 8 we will offer signposts and practical suggestions for different stepping stones that can help a team take the necessary risks together to deepen their understanding and to truly embed and sustain the change they wish to make. As a general note we strongly recommend using the same games with staff teams as would be used to practice and teach the skills with children. This is not to patronise or demean early years colleagues, indeed we use lots of these games in our training to both demonstrate practical ideas for children as well as providing a level of experiential learning that often deepens awareness and cohesion in a group. It is an easy route in changing practice by introducing and play new games as a staff team where the objective and reasoning is to rehearse something new to try with children. In the process staff are also connecting with each other and explicitly practicing and experiencing using the skills together. Playing the games in this way works at two levels of professional practice: (1) with children and (2) for the staff team.

An important reminder – it's about being a team and owning a vision

Are you a team or just a group of individuals working in the same place?

Being a team is more than group of people brought together working in the same physical space and location. The relationships and skills that characterise a team include how and where a group of people to connect, challenge and support each other so that both individually and as an organisation they can achieve more.

Various factors can prevent a group of people flourishing and coming together as a team; interpersonal dynamics, turnover of staff, stress and heavy workloads are some of the ways teams can become fragmented and struggle. Furthermore, as we identified in Chapter 2, where conflict is not expressed, remains hidden or is destructive rather than constructive, then this too can severely limit a team and what it can achieve for an organization.

Mirroring the same group dynamic progression and relational process as the children, trust is a key starting point for bringing a team together, breaking down barriers and laying the groundwork for professional relationships and connections that include everyone.

Simple activities and games can break the ice and achieve this in a non-threatening way for staff, as we have set out with some suggestions below.

Practical suggestions:

- Try the same games for eye contact and knowing and using names, as recommended for using with children
- Discuss ground rules as team for expectations around how people will behave and contribute to staff meetings
- Rather than always sitting in the same place, next to the same people, get staff moving around and sitting somewhere different and next to someone new every staff meeting.

Sharing a vision – and agreeing your goals and priorities

We are repeating ourselves again here, but that is because we believe so strongly how important a shared vision is for an early years setting. Setting aside a staff meeting, staff training or away day is time well spent and invested when staff have the opportunity to talk together about their vision for the organization. Beyond their busy day to day demands they can reflect, remind and affirm deeper motivations and aspirations, such as, why is this early years setting here? What are we all about? What do we want to achieve? What do we want for our children, families and community?

People can have their own aspirations and goals for what they want to achieve in a setting. What is fundamental is that this is not in contradiction with a shared vision that everyone buys in on and subscribes to. Where this shared ownership of vision as a team is in place further discussions, sharing and agreement can be established around priorities, goals and decisions around ways forward as an organization. Moreover, this also provides a secure framework and rationale to support the whole staff team in taking responsibility not just for oneself but each other as well; it opens the door for exploring avenues of holding each other accountable and focusing on results, both of which are features of higher functioning teams (Lencioni, 2005). Before we investigate practical ways of developing such mastery in teams we relocate teams back to the first steps of trust. In Chapter 8 we considered how an individual early years practitioner can build trust with colleagues, families and children through practical strategies such as improving eye contact and knowing and using names.

Discussing and setting these goals and expectations as a staff team can benefit an early years setting in a number of ways:

- It brings a whole staff team on board, setting clear expectations and the same message for everyone
- Develops consistency in professional practice which is great modeling for the children to see and develop the same skills
- Enables staff to support each other
- Through their interactions and practising of the skills it builds trust across the team.

In introducing games to play and explicitly intentionally addressing each of these skills, leaders and managers in early years can take practical steps to building trust among a team. This also provides an opening for staff to reflect together and a safe environment where they can begin to develop sufficient trust and confidence to engage in more risky conversations about how they are working together as part of their professional practice. For some teams and settings, first gentle steps such as these and general reflections on trust in a team can be very scary and uncomfortable.

Leaders and managers of early years settings need to remain sensitive to where their staff are and reflect on how they can be challenged without alienating or freaking them out.

Building on smaller steps to more challenging ones

Where practical steps to building trust helps a team take its first steps towards developing assertiveness, we now consider how teams can take a bigger leap forward together in confronting and addressing their communication together, particularly around conflict.

1. Encourage and value constructive conflict and disagreement

Early years teams often struggle to feel comfortable with conflict and embrace it as a positive benefit for working together (Ota and Vollick, 2011). We have seen how frequently conflict, disagreement and anger can remain hidden and, where expressed, is diminishing and destructive for a team. So how can a team move forward from here?

Have the conversation and bring it into the open

A first key step is to bring the topic of conflict and constructive conflict into the open and get a team talking about it together. After making an initial case for why conflict, the right kind of conflict (see Chapter 2), has an important role to play for effective teams, it can be helpful to encourage team members to reflect on their own general attitudes to conflict and how they cope with it.

To reiterate, how these conversations are structured and how questions are asked requires sensitivity and a careful attention to the climate and trust among team members. Early years leaders and managers or other professionals leading the session should remain mindful of group dynamics and use strategies that encourage all members to participate and share their thoughts and feelings. This can be achieved by:

- working in pairs or small groups and feeding back to the larger group
- using post sticks for each team member to note their own idea or thought and lay them all out together, possibly grouping common themes and ideas, the further discussion and consideration

- depending on the size of the team, going round each person in turn to contribute an opinion, feeling or idea.

Considering each individuals' story of conflict

A useful question to ask for generating discussion is for the team to reflect on their own experiences of conflict growing up and in their families. Invariably when reflecting on their experiences as a child, individuals can become more aware of their own approach to conflict in the present, recognizing the significant role their experience as a child plays in how they feel about conflict and how they cope with it in the present day. As with all discussions around conflict and other sensitive topics, in setting boundaries and expectations for this activity it is worth reminding everyone that this is a general discussion and not an extensive therapy session. In our experience this gentle reminder helps people frame their discussion and reflections in an appropriate way.

Creating a Team Agreement for Conflict

Where staff are able to engage positively and listen to each other in this task there is a further opportunity to build greater trust, create more understanding and empathy between colleagues and deeper appreciation and acceptance of diversity and how differently people come to situations of conflict. From this there is a springboard for bringing individual experiences and perspectives together to form an agreed team approach to conflict. Lencioni proposes a discussion around setting out acceptable and unacceptable behaviours that are relevant, meaningful and pertinent to each individual team (2005). The process of having such conversations as a team in itself can do much to help staff shift more positively towards confronting conflict; encouraging further empathy, understanding and confidence in an environment of mutual trust, support and respect.

Once an initial proposal acceptable and unacceptable behaviours is set out, and it needs only three or four simply worded agreements as an initial starting point. This in itself marks a significant movement for a team. Having clear parameters agreed and clearly laid out means that there is explicit guidance on how to enter into and behave during difficult conversations in situations of conflict. It also means that colleagues can further support and remind each other, in addition to holding each other accountable if they are not engaging with conflict according to an agreed team code.

2. Become more aware of the assumptions we use

Case study

Lucy has been quiet all morning and not her usual chatty, cheery self. In fact at break time Sarah was sure she gave her a funny look and had been talking about her when she walked into the staff room for her tea break. Sarah talks to her friend later and having thought and dwelt on it all afternoon, is now convinced Lucy is annoyed with her over something and doesn't like her.

Discussion

Everyday we all make assumptions about the world around us and the people we meet. To help us process and understand what we are experiencing, assumptions have an important role on helping us make sense of what is happening, what we are hearing and seeing. In this scenario Sarah is making lots of assumptions about what Lucy is talking about and how she is feeling about Sarah. When Sarah speaks to her friend later in the afternoon, she tells her friend that Lucy is annoyed with her and doesn't like her. If we pause here, we notice that with the information we have there is no way of knowing this and there are many reasons why Lucy might be quiet and acting like she is, none of which could have anything to do with Sarah or how Lucy feels about Sarah. For example, Lucy may be experiencing difficulties at home, she may be feeling unwell or simply just tired.

Like Sarah in the above scenario, people generally work and live with their assumptions about life, people and the world without really questioning or being aware of them. Sometimes our assumptions are just that, an assumption – a conjecture, a supposition or an inference – rather than something we actually, concretely know is true as fact. It is when we act on a mistaken belief, or incorrect assumption, that problems can arise.

If we return to Sarah's assumptions about Lucy, Sarah can't really know what is going on unless she asks Lucy. She needs to check in with Lucy and might say something like,

> Lucy, you seem very quiet and I got the impression at break time that you weren't very happy with me. Is there anything I've done to upset you or is there anything else going on?

From here Lucy has the opportunity to clarify the situation and Sarah will now know what the situation is, instead of presuming and thinking she knows by making a series of assumptions.

It is valuable to remind ourselves about the assumptions we make from time to time, making us more aware of whether we really know something is true or we are just speculating. Early years colleagues and teams, like all of us, operate with assumptions and so it can be valuable to think about the assumptions colleagues might have about each other, as well as the children and families in their setting.

Greater awareness of how we use assumptions can help with more effective assertiveness communication; in step one of the three steps assertiveness (what happened, the facts), it is not what we think happened, or our interpretation of it, but what actually happened, the concrete facts.

3. Explore the basics of difficult conversations together as a team

Interwoven with the more challenging steps of considering constructive conflict and assumptions, the acknowledgement of difficult conversations is a further avenue that can help support and move a team forward in developing assertive communication. Difficult conversations can be different things for different people; for some it might be addressing professional practice with a colleague, whilst for others it could be engaging with more personal problems such as illness of a family member or bereavement. Whatever the topic a difficult conversation, like conflict, is uncomfortable. Beyond this though, is the issue of whether they have to happen.

This is where the foundation of a shared, agreed vision is useful; if everyone on a team has agreed on a vision, anything that is not congruent with this should be challenged and the person held accountable, regardless of anyone's position or role in the organisation.

Staff teams can be supported in exploring difficult conversations by considering why, like constructive conflict, they are important and practical strategies for how they can be handled. We frequently find that many practitioners want practical ideas and a deeper understanding of difficult conversations. There is more we could discuss that is beyond the space we have here but for the purposes of this book we would suggest that a few key messages and topics for discussion around difficult conversations may focus on:

(1) That everyone has a choice – you can have them, or not have them.
(2) There are consequences, whatever you decide – if you don't have the conversation you may well end up only postponing it until the situation has to be addressed some time later (when it may have escalated and got even worse).
(3) Every member of the team has a responsibility to the children, colleagues and the setting, it is part of their role and responsibilities to have them.
(4) Whilst a person might not like having difficult conversations they can take practical steps to help themselves to prepare, such as:

(a) considering their motivations
(b) asking what they want or don't want as an outcome
(c) recognizing their feelings and trying to stay calm
(d) during the conversation staying focused on the topic (not getting distracted) and making sure at the end they summarise, clarify and agree a way forward/next step.

The three steps of assertive communication are a useful tool to use as part of difficult conversations at work.

Again the process of talking together as a team about the topic can contribute to a safer a more trusting environment. In sharing thoughts and feelings, colleagues can become more empathic and understanding of each other. With expectations established and permission, as well as support, given, staff can help each other initiate such conversations together. This is not only about the person raising the issue, but also how the person receiving the message responds and is willing to engage in the dialogue.

We have considered a number of different ways in which early years leaders and managers can introduce the broader landscape of constructive conflict, assumptions and difficult conversations as part of developing assertive communication in a setting and with an early years team. We now move on to explore different ways assertiveness itself can be introduced and developed with a team.

Ready for assertiveness?

Across the chapters of this book we have set out the theoretical background behind assertiveness, as well as some suggested practical steps for using assertive communication in early years settings. The ideas, concepts and strategies presented can be used by any early years practitioner and in justifying the many benefits of this type of communication, we have also highlighted how assertiveness can be developed and embedded as a whole team approach.

The three steps to assertiveness that we have laid out provide a vocabulary and accessible framework for all staff to engage with the ideas and concept. Our other discussions (Chapters 7 and 8) have broken down each of these three steps into further stepping stones for building knowledge, understanding and skills. For the early years manager who is committed to developing and introducing assertive communication into their setting we offer the following signposts and suggestions for introducing assertiveness to an early years team.

(1) Start by getting the conversation going – compare assertiveness with aggressive, passive and passive aggressive communication.

(2) Break down three steps and explore each element further by taking a specific goal to work on e.g. extending emotional vocabulary, identifying how you are feeling, practicing say 'I feel . . . '.

(3) Consider what its like receiving assertive communication and explore active listening skills.

(4) Investigate nonverbal communication together, both for assertive communication and communication generally to raise awareness and enable staff to give feedback to each other on how they communicate with each other.

(5) Bring the three steps together – use different scenarios and practice structuring and saying phrases that use the three steps assertiveness framework.

(6) Agree how as a team you are going to support each other – encouraging colleagues' attempts to use assertiveness, patience, tolerance, not accepting other more destructive kinds of conflict and communication (e.g. speaking behind a colleagues back, passive aggressive communication).

(7) Familiar, comfortable communication habits can be hard to break and honestly communicating what we think, feel and want can be very daunting (Dryden and Constantinou, 2004) so start with agreeing small, realistic goals. Before tackling more challenging situations or people (at home or work) encourage staff to practise and try out strategies with other friends and family members they feel safe with, or when returning an item to a shop.

(8) Have a plan – talk about it, review it and hold each other accountable – once embarking on this path together its important to let it slide, leave it off the agenda or allow other matters knock it into the background. A plan helps, set and agree goals as a team for where you want to be and what you are going to try together by next week, by the end of the month and where you want to be at the end

of the year. You can then keep returning to this to assess where you are, what you need to keep moving and celebrating your success.

(9) Give it time – as with all kinds of change in any organization, it takes time and ongoing follow up for longer term sustainability and embedding into professional practice as a whole setting approach.

(10) Make it part of your vision – many early years settings describe their values and vision around principles of equality, diversity, belonging, inclusion, valuing and respect, independence and taking responsibility for oneself and others. The knowledge, skills and understanding of assertive communication is apposite as a practical and reliable way of translating those principles into everyday actions, words and relationships.

Concluding remarks

We contend that there is a strong and convincing case for bringing assertive communication to early years teams and settings. For individual early years practitioners it provides it gives a boost to self-esteem and confidence that comes from being to stand up for yourself; it supports and enables difficult conversations and constructive conflict which is an inevitable and important component for early years settings and teams to grow and improve.

For assertiveness to flourish and benefit the organization we do not propose a one day staff training is enough. It is instead an ethos, a commitment to professional relationships and accountability. Broad and strong foundations need to be in place to support and help teams take the necessary risks to change and try out new ways of talking and being.

The good news is that a collaborative, team effort is the most effective and easiest way of achieving change. Anchored in a strong, shared vision for themselves and their children and in an environment of mutual trust, openness and support assertiveness will be encouraged, sustained and thereby strengthen and advance the individual, the team and the setting.

References

Dryden, W. and Constantinou, D. (2004) *Assertiveness – step by step*, London, Sheldon Press.

Lencioni, P. (2005) *Overcoming the five dysfunctions of a team – a field guide*, San Francisco: Jossey Bass.

Ota, C. and Vollick, M. P. (2011) 'Inspiring values, skills, confidence and communities – a case study of a social, relational approach to religious education and spirituality in the early years', *Journal of Religious Education* 59(2): 23–34.

Index